2nd Edition

THE
VISION
OF
MODERN
DANCE

2nd Edition

THE
VISION
OF
MODERN
DANCE
In the Words of Its Creators

Edited by
Jean Morrison Brown
Naomi Mindlin
and Charles H. Woodford

Princeton Book Company, Publishers
Hightstown, New Jersey

To Those With Vision

Copyright © 1979, 1998 by
Princeton Book Company, Publishers
All rights reserved
Library of Congress Catalog Card Number 97–28330
ISBN 0–87127–205–9
Printed in the United States of America

Cover photo by Tom Brazil of Nina Watt in
Doris Humphrey's *The Call/Breath of Fire*

The vision of modern dance: in the words of its creators/edited by Jean
    Morrison Brown, Naomi Mindlin, and Charles H. Woodford.—
    2nd ed.
            p.   cm.
    Includes bibliographical references (p.) and index.
    ISBN 0–87127–205–9 (alk. paper)
    1. Modern dance. 2. Dancers—Biography. I. Brown, Jean
Morrison. II. Mindlin, Naomi, 1948–   . III. Woodford, Charles
Humphrey.
GV1783.V57   1997
792.8′092′2—dc21   97-28330
                                                              CIP

Acknowledgments

Isadora Duncan. *The Art of the Dance.* New York: Theatre Arts Books, 1928. *My Life,* New York: Liveright Publishing Corporation, 1927. Unpublished manuscript, Harvard University Theatre Collection. WNET Great Performances: Dance in America, *Trailblazers of Modern Dance,* 1977.

Loïe Fuller. "Light and the Dance." In Fuller, *Fifteen Years of A Dancer's Life.* Boston: Small, Maynard & Co., Inc., 1913. Reprint. Brooklyn: Dance Horizons, 1976.

Ted Shawn. "Constants—What Constitutes a Work of Art in the Dance." In Shawn, *Dance We Must.* Pittsfield, MA: The Eagle Printing & Binding Co., 1940, 1950, 1963. Reprint. New York: Haskell House, 1974.

Mary Wigman. "Stage Dance-Stage Dancer (1927)." In Wigman, *The Mary Wigman Book.* Edited and translated by Walter Sorell. Middletown, CT: Wesleyan University Press, 1975. Copyright © by Walter Sorell, by permission of Wesleyan University Press.

Martha Graham. "Graham 1937." In Merle Armitage, ed., *Martha Graham.* Los Angeles: privately printed, 1937. Reprint. Brooklyn: Dance Horizons, 1966.

Doris Humphrey. "What a Dancer Thinks About." Unpublished manuscript. Dance Collection, New York Public Library at Lincoln Center.

Charles Weidman. "Random Remarks." In Walter Sorell, ed., *The Dance Has Many Faces.* 2d ed. rev. New York: Columbia University Press, 1966.

Hanya Holm. "Hanya Speaks." In Walter Sorell, *Hanya Holm: Biography of an Artist.* Middletown, CT: Wesleyan University Press, 1969. Copyright © 1969 by Wesleyan University, by permission of Wesleyan University Press.

Merce Cunningham. "You have to love dancing to stick to it." In Cunningham, *Changes: Notes on Choreography.* New York: Something Else Press, 1968. Copyright © 1968 by Merce Cunningham.

Erick Hawkins. "a little house to understand and protect it." *Dance Observer* 27, no. 2 (1960).

José Limón. "On Dance." In Fernando Puma, ed., *Seven Arts #1.* Garden City, NY: Doubleday & Co., Inc., 1953.

Anna Sokolow. "The Rebel and the Bourgeois." In Selma Jeanne Cohen, ed., *The Modern Dance: Seven Statements of Belief.* Middletown, CT: Wesleyan University Press, 1965. Copyright ©; 1965 by Wesleyan University, reprinted by permission of Wesleyan University Press.

Alwin Nikolais. Excerpts from "Nik: A Documenary." Edited by Marcia B. Siegel. *Dance Perspectives* 48 (1971). Copyright © 1971 by Dance Perspectives Foundation. Reprinted with permission.

Paul Taylor. Excerpt from *Private Domain*. New York: Alfred A. Knopf, 1987. Copyright © 1987 by Paul Taylor, reprinted by permission of Alfred A. Knopf, Inc.

Alvin Ailey. Excerpt from Alvin Ailey and A. Peter Bailey, *Revelations*. New York: Carol Publishing Group, 1995. Copyright © 1995, reprinted with permission of Carol Publishing Group.

Anna Halprin. "The Process is the Purpose." An interview with Vera Maletic. *Dance Scope* 4, no. 1 (1967–1968) Copyright © 1968 American Dance Guild.

Judith Dunn. "We Don't Talk about It. We Engage in It." *Eddy* 1, no. 2 (1974).

Yvonne Rainer. "The Mind is a Muscle." *Work* 1961–73. Halifax: The Press of The Nova Scotia College of Art and Design; New York: New York University Press, 1974.

Pilobolus. "Talking with Pilobolus." An interview with Elvi Moore. *Dance Scope* 10, no. 2 (1976). Copyright © 1976 by American Dance Guild.

Trisha Brown and Douglas Dunn. "Dialogue: On Dance." *Performing Arts Journal* 1, no. 2 (1976).

Rod Rodgers. "Don't Tell Me Who I Am." *Negro Digest* 18, 1968.

Twyla Tharp. Excerpt from *Push Comes to Shove* by Twyla Tharp. New York: Bantam Books, 1992. Copyright © 1992 by Twyla Tharp. Used by permission of Bantam Books, a division of Doubleday Dell Publishing Group, Inc.

Mark Morris. Excerpt from Thea Singer, "Mark Morris: Beautiful Dancers." *Stuff Magazine* #113 (June 1992). Copyright © 1992 by Thea Singer, reprinted with permission of Thea Singer.

Childs, Lucinda, and Sophie Constanti. "Against the Tide." *Dance Theatre Journal* 8, no. 4 (Spring 1991): 6–8.

Dufton, Merry. "Eiko and Koma interview." *New Dance* 43 (January 1988): 15–17.

Fulkerson, Mary. "BITS: A post-modern acculumation process." *Contact Quarterly* 12, no. 3 (Fall 1987): 39–41.

Gordon, David, Nancy Stark Smith and Valda Setterfield. "David Gordon & Valda Setterfield Talk about Labels, Madmen, Vanity and more." *Contact Quarterly* 4, no. 2 (Winter 1979): 5–8.

Fenley, Molissa, and Alexandra Grilikhes. "Beginning with Ritual." *Dance Now* 4, no. 2 (Summer 1995): 31–37.

Hay, Deborah. "Remaining Positionless." *Contact Quarterly* 13, no. 2 (Spring/Summer 1988): 22–23.

Jones, Bill T., Mary Overlie and Steve Paxton. "The Studies Project." *Contact Quarterly* 9, no. 3 (Fall 1984): 30–37.

Mason, Francis. "A Conversation with Garth Fagan." *Ballet Review* 23, no. 1 (Spring 1995): 19–28.

Zollar, Jowale Willa Jo, and Tess Triumph. "Jowale Willa Jo Zollar interviewed by Tessa Triumph." *New Dance* 41 (Summer 1987): 10–14.

Photographs

From the archives of the Dance Collection of the New York Public
Library at Lincoln Center:

Isadora Duncan, photographer unknown
Loïe Fuller in *Serpentine Dance,* drawing by Toulouse-Lautrec
Ruth St. Denis in *Incense,* photographer unknown
Ted Shawn in *Frohsinn,* photographer unknown
Mary Wigman in "Schwingende Landschaft" from *Sommerlicher
    Tanz,* photograph by Charlotte Rudolph
Martha Graham in *Cave of the Heart,* photographer unknown
Charles Weidman, photographer unknown
Hanya Holm in *Icon,* photograph by Charlotte Rudolph
Erick Hawkins in *John Brown,* photograph by Alfredo Valente
José Limón, photograph by Zachary Freyman, by permission
    of the photographer
Anna Sokolow, photographer unknown
Alwin Nikolais, photograph by Basil Langton
Pilobolus in *Monkshood Farewell,* photographer unknown
Trisha Brown, photographer unknown

By permission of Charles Humphrey Woodford:
    Doris Humphrey in *Theater Piece,* photographer unknown
By permission of the Cunningham Dance Foundation:
    Merce Cunningham, photograph by Penny Brogden
Courtesy of Paul Taylor Dance Company:
    Paul Taylor in *Epic,* photograph by Robert Rauschenberg
By permission of Dance Theater Foundation, Inc.:
    Alvin Ailey, photograph by Normand Maxon
By permission of Anna Halprin:
    Anna Halprin, photographer unknown
By permission of Douglas Dunn:
    Douglas Dunn, photographer unknown
By permission of Rod Rodgers:
    Rod Rodgers, photographer unknown
By permission of Greg Gorman:
    Twyla Tharp, photograph by Greg Gorman
By permission of Chantal Regnault:
    Mark Morris, photograph by Chantal Regnault

PREFACE

The history of modern dance is one of strong-minded, independent individuals. The leaders of each succeeding generation, in breaking away from their mentors, created according to their own personalities and times. When these new leaders became established, they in turn became the focus of rebellion by younger dancers, often their company members, who began to choreograph, develop their own techniques and means of artistic expression in movement, and establish their own schools and companies. As a result, the newest modern dance remains true to the spirit of innovation that motivated its originators, although its external form has changed drastically.

In the early days, the search was to gain, in the words of Louis Horst, "inner sensitivity to every one of the body's parts, to the power of its whole and to the space in which it carves designs. The great quest was to find ways to attain this sensitivity and manners in which to discipline it for communication." This was the heritage of the originators, carried on and furthered by their successors.

The evolution of American modern dance over the last seventy-five years reflects conceptual changes that can be found in all the arts. In some cases there has been direct and significant mutual exchange between dancers and other artists. Like the contemporary trends in the other arts, modern dance affords creative individuality through wide-ranging subject matter. The continuing rebellion against the traditional past, as a renewing self-assertion, has brought forth the highly individual statements that characterize the works of present-day artists.

The aesthetics of modern dance lies in the integration of movement and meaning through three-dimensional kinetic design, which is restricted only by the anatomical limits of the human body and the artist's conceptualization. Even at its most expressive, dance is nonliteral, employing abstractions and exaggerations of movement to create an illusion in time-space through the use of force. Spatial design is realized in part by plastic positioning and in part by trace designs created through movement of parts or of the whole body. Rhythmic design is achieved by time-force interactions in space, creating dynamics.

Because dance is a time-space, nonverbal art, many dancers do not express themselves readily in words. Others, however, are most articulate. The early modem dancers seem to have felt an especially strong need to give verbal expression to their beliefs.

The selections presented here are dancers' statements of their philosophies. They span the historical scope of modern dance, from those who paved the way for its development to the present, and reveal the overall changes in modem dance during the twentieth century, which have nevertheless occurred within the framework of a common theoretical outlook. In many cases, a statement, although written at an early period in the artist's development, reflects a philosophy that, in essence, remained unchanged during the course of his or her career. Others simply express a position at one point in the artist's development. Many important dancers are not included, primarily because they have been too busy with dance and dancing to write about it.

—Jean Morrison Brown, 1979

* * *

In the eighteen years since publication of the first edition of this book, modern dance has reached a wider audience than its originators ever dreamed possible. Credit for this can go to TV programs such as *Dance in America,* the release of videos, an increase in North American modern dance companies, and international growth. German modern dance, thought to have disappeared with World War II, has rebounded with vigor, while new companies have formed in other European countries as well as in Asia, Australia, and South America. (Anyone interested in an overview of recent developments in central Europe should view the video *European Dance Theater,* released by Dance Horizons. For a comprehensive history of the international scope of modern dance, read *Art Without Boundaries* by Jack Anderson.)

Numerically, the audience for a live modern dance company has probably never surpassed Denishawn, with its crowd-pleasing, cross-country tours in the 1920s and trans-Asian tour of 1925-26. The concert dancers of the 1930s and later, performing in New York City or in colleges on "the gymnasium circuit," reached a smaller number of people—often educators, students, intellectuals, and other artists.

The Vision of Modern Dance is for this same audience, especially for students who may wish to become dancers or choreographers. For anyone, it provides a succinct narrative history, combined with origi-

nal statements by the dancers themselves, as a way to better understand the art form. It purposely does not contain a single word of
dance criticism so that the reader may form an opinion based solely
on original writings. Of course, a full understanding of dance requires
seeing it, and it is hoped that the reader will attend performances and
view videos. (A videography is provided at the end of the book for
videos that are in circulation as of this writing, but the reader should
also consult *Dance on Camera: A Guide to Dance Films and Videos*
[Scarecrow Press, 1997] and the internet.)

As an aside, it is interesting to note that modern dance began at the
same time as silent movies—when people were becoming used to
seeing expressive movement and gesture without the benefit of dialogue, and with one or more musicians playing background music.
Both Louis Horst, Martha Graham's mentor, and Denishawn dancer
Pauline Lawrence (later Mrs. José Limón) began their careers as
pianists in movie theaters, and the Denishawn Company itself
appeared in Hollywood-made silent films. With the advent of TV, followed by videos, the public eye became accustomed to a daily diet of
moving visual images. The popularity of dance concerts began to
boom. Recently, the combination of video and dance spawned a new
experimental art: videodance.

Updates and corrections have been made throughout the Second
Edition, noting death dates for several choreographers and the next
chapter in the careers of others. Additions include selections by Paul
Taylor, Alvin Ailey, Twyla Tharp, and Mark Morris, as well as brief
statements by nine contemporary choreographers. The final chapter,
The New Vision, is introduced by author Don McDonagh in his role
as an observer.

In the first edition of *The Vision of Modern Dance,* Jean Morrision
Brown thanked the following people: Professor David Magidson,
Professor Allegra Fuller Snyder, Professor Emma Lewis Thomas,
Professor Louis Hudon, Genevieve Oswald and the staff of the Dance
Collection of the New York Public Library at Lincoln Center, the staff
of the Harvard Theatre Collection at Harvard University, Susan
Edwards, Joanna Gewertz Harris, Eleanor Lauer, Ernestine Stodelle,
Marian Van Tuyl, Theodora Wiesner, Deborah Jackson, and Charles
Woodford. I would like to thank the following people for their help
in the research for this second edition: Leslie Getz, Douglas Dunn,
Anna Halprin, Claudia Gitelman, Murray Louis, Rod Rodgers, and
Lorry May.

—Charles H. Woodford, 1997

TABLE OF CONTENTS

Part One

THE FORERUNNERS

INTRODUCTION

Modern dance is usually regarded as a uniquely American, twentieth-century art form. However, as all rebellions evolve from precedents, so the antecedents of modern dance can be found in nineteenth-century Europe.

The French singer François Delsarte (1811-1871) delineated basic principles of movement and expression in movement. His theory, formulated in the *Science of Applied Aesthetics,* divided the body into three zones, with each zone further divided into three sections for the purpose of expressive gesture. Movements were assigned to one of three basic categories: successions, parallelisms, and oppositions. These theories were originally developed for actors and musicians, but they later reached dancers through the efforts of his disciples and ultimately revolutionized dance.

Emile Jaques-Dalcroze (1865-1950) was born in Vienna but performed his major work in Geneva. He developed a system of rhythmic exercises called *Eurythmics,* which were designed to foster music students' expressivity by creating a greater feeling for the movement inherent in the music. His connection with Delsarte is uncertain, but exposure to Delsartean theories seems probable. Early modern dancers studied Eurythmics in order to foster rhythmic sensitivity.

Rudolf von Laban (1879-1958), the son of a Hungarian diplomat, studied with a disciple of Delsarte and is reported to have studied ballet as well. He established a school in Switzerland and then one in Germany, where he trained movement choirs until 1938, when he moved to England. He invented a notation system called *Labanotation,* now widely used in recording and reconstructing choreography. His *Effort-Shape* theories have been incorporated into dance education and dance therapy, while his space concepts may still be seen in the work of dancers who carry on the tradition of German modern dance.

In America, disciples of Delsarte, including Genevieve

Stebbins, Steele Mackaye, and Mrs. Richard Hovey, taught his work in the late nineteenth century. Stebbins studied in Europe with a disciple of Delsarte, then toured the U. S., giving lecture-demonstrations while dressed in a Greek tunic. Mackaye studied with Delsarte himself and then developed the principles into a system of exercises called *Harmonic Gymnastics*. A Delsarte craze ensued throughout America. Mrs. Richard Hovey studied in France with Delsarte's son, Gustave, who had evolved a movement system similar to Mackaye's. These disciples and others influenced the American dancers who created the climate out of which American modern dance eventually arose.

Isadora Duncan and Ruth St. Denis were born at about the same time (1877–1878) on opposite sides of the American continent. Both had dominant, liberated mothers who imparted to them the principles of François Delsarte; both had brief stints in show business before traveling to Europe; and both were influenced by Loïe Fuller, another American dancer, who was the rage of the Folies Bergère.

The rebelliousness that has characterized the leaders of modern dance has its origins in the work of St. Denis, Duncan, and Fuller. At a time when women were corseted, disenfranchised, and denied access to education and jobs, these three women lived a liberated existence and expressed a freedom in their art that relatively few other women possessed. They freed their bodies by discarding the conventions of Victorian costume; they sought to synthesize movement and expression. In short, they sought individuality.

Both Duncan and St. Denis opened their minds by reading and doing research in museums as well as by traveling extensively. Images from the past inspired both with visions of the future of dance, and both expressed their philosophies in writing. The followers of Isadora Duncan inherited a style and a point of view that has had a far-reaching influence on American modern dance, as has the legacy of Ruth St. Denis, which became meshed with that of Ted Shawn.

At the time that Duncan, St. Denis, and Fuller were liberating themselves through dance and winning public esteem, dance was still a taboo profession for American men. It took courage for

Ted Shawn, a former divinity student, to become a dancer. He first toured the vaudeville circuit. Although he had seen Ruth St. Denis dance in 1911, it was not until 1914 that he auditioned for her and became her partner, and then her husband. In 1915 the couple founded Denishawn, a school that dominated American theatrical dancing for the next fifteen years.

Oriental dance and ballet were taught at the school, as well as yoga, Delsartean theories (taught to Ted Shawn during this period by Mrs. Hovey), and a wide variety of ethnic dance styles. The dances choreographed by St. Denis and Shawn reflected the philosophy of the school: expressive, eclectic works on ethnic and/or religious themes that treated existing dance forms in new ways.

At the height of its success, the Los Angeles-based Denishawn franchised schools from coast to coast, which were run by former students. There were also two touring companies, one directed by "Miss Ruth" and the other by Shawn. Men were included in both the schools and the companies, for one of Shawn's ambitions was to restore to male dancing the respect it had commanded in ancient Greece.

Although Denishawn encompassed all forms of dancing, the vision of its founders fell short of accepting diverging theories. Their blindness to innovation on the part of company members, together with personal difficulties and unrealistic expectations for a "Greater Denishawn"* in the year of the stock market crash, eventually led to Denishawn's demise.

During this same period Mary Wigman established her school of German modern dance in Dresden, Germany, in 1920. She had studied with both Dalcroze and Laban, and she strongly influenced the course of German modern dance for the next fifty years. Branches of the school were set up throughout Germany, with a New York branch established in 1931 (directed by Hanya Holm), following her first American tour. She undertook her third and final American tour with her company in 1933.

---

*"Greater Denishawn" encompassed a vision of expansion which took the form of plans for centers on both the East and West coasts.

EXCERPTS FROM
HER WRITINGS

Isadora Duncan
1877–1927

*I*sadora Duncan had a tremendous and long-range impact on
dancers, artists, and society as a whole. A feminist in the most
contemporary sense of the word and a radical whose rebellion,
particularly against ballet, was complete and far-reaching, she was also
a Romantic. The writings of Nietzsche, Rousseau, and Walt Whitman
influenced her greatly, and she performed to the music of Gluck,
Wagner, Schubert, and Chopin, among others.

Isadora believed that dance should come from and be an expression
of the spirit, inspired by nature; anything else was stilted and artificial.
She felt that her philosophy was best exemplified in ancient Greek civilization, and her basic costume was a Greek tunic.

She found little acceptance in her native country. From 1899, she
lived and performed in Europe, where she enjoyed sensational success,
especially in Russia. She inspired artists, poets, and musicians. In 1908
and again in 1914 she returned to the United States to perform, but
Americans disapproved of the liberated life style that pervaded her art.

In spite of her several attempts to establish schools in Germany,
France, and Russia to continue her vision, Isadora's lifelong dream was
repeatedly frustrated. Part of the difficulty was financial; part was her
unwillingness to systematize her art and her inability to transmit her
spirit; part was her frequent absence from the school. However, the
essence of her vision and her rebellion remains with us, and continues
to influence dancers today.

In a moment of prophetic love for America, Walt Whitman said: "I hear America singing," and I can imagine the mighty song that Walt heard from the surge of the Pacific over the plains, the voices rising of the vast Choral of children, youths, men and women, singing Democracy.

When I read this poem of Whitman's I, too, had a vision— the vision of America dancing a dance that would be the worthy expression of the song Walt heard when he heard America singing. It would have nothing to do with the sensual lilt of the jazz rhythm: it would be like the vibration of the American soul striving upward, through labour to harmonious life. Nor had this dance that I visioned any vestige of the Foxtrot or the Charleston—rather was it the living leap of the child springing toward the heights, towards its future accomplishment, towards a new great vision of life that would express America.

I see America dancing, standing with one foot poised on the highest point of the Rockies, her two hands stretched from the Atlantic to the Pacific, her fine head tossed to the sky, her forehead shining with a Crown of a million stars.

* * *

I was born by the sea . . . my first idea of movement of the dance, certainly came from the rhythm of the waves. . . .

* * *

The great and only principle on which I feel myself justified in leaning, is a constant, absolute, and universal unity which runs through all the manifestations of Nature. The waters, the winds, the plants, living creatures, the particles of matter itself obey this controlling rhythm of which the characteristic line is the wave. In nothing does Nature suggest jumps and breaks, there is between all the conditions of life a continuity or flow which the dancer must respect in his art, or else become a mannequin—outside Nature and without true beauty.

* * *

It is the alternate attraction and resistance of the law of gravity that causes this wave movement.

* * *

Every movement that can be danced on the seashore, without being in harmony with the rhythm of the waves, every movement that can be danced in the forest without being in harmony with the swaying of the branches, every movement that one can dance nude, in the sunshine, in the open country, without being in harmony with the life and the solitude of the landscape—every such movement is false, in that it is out of tune in the midst of Nature's harmonious lines. That is why the dancer should above all else choose movements that express the strength, health, nobility, ease and serenity of living things.

* * *

When I have danced I have tried always to be the Chorus; I have been the Chorus of young girls hailing the return of the fleet; I have been the Chorus dancing the Pyrrhic Dance, or the Bacchic; I have never once danced a solo.

* * *

Now, I am going to reveal to you something which is very pure, a totally white thought. It is always in my heart; it blooms at each of my steps. . . . The dance is love, it is only love, it alone, and that is enough. . . . I then, it is amorously that I dance; to poems, to music, but now I would like to no longer dance to anything but the rhythm of my soul.

* * *

Is it not true that all the graces of God are upon woman . . . that all the marvelous litheness of the animal, that the gestures of the flower are in her? So, if she has all the gifts, she is the reflection of the world. She is also like a garland suspended between reality and the ideal. . . . She can, with all her gestures, represent all ideas. If the gesture is right, the idea is beautiful.

She is the proud huntress, the virgin Walkyrie, Botticelli's Spring, the lascivious nymph, the intoxicated Bacchante,

Antigone in tears, the mother at the cradle, the supplicant at the altar, the priestess in the sacred grove, the lewd and the chaste. . . . Finally, she is a fresco of changing grace, her body floats and undulates like silk in the wind, princess of rhythms performing the dance in the garden of life.

* * *

Oh, what a field is here awaiting her! Do you not feel that she is near, that she is coming, this dancer of the future! She will help womankind to a new knowledge of the possible strength and beauty of their bodies, and the relation of their bodies to the earth nature and to the children of the future. She will dance the body emerging again from centuries of civilized forgetfulness, emerging not in the nudity of primitive man, but in a new nakedness, no longer at war with spirituality and intelligence, but joining with them in a glorious harmony.

This is the mission of the dancer of the future. Oh, do you not feel that she is near, do you not long for her coming as I do? Let us prepare the place for her. I would build for her a temple to await her. Perhaps she is yet unborn, perhaps she is now a little child. Perhaps, oh blissful! it may be my holy mission to guide her first steps, to watch the progress of her movements day by day until, far outgrowing my poor teaching, her movements will become godlike, mirroring in themselves the waves, the winds, the movements of growing things, the flight of birds, the passing of clouds, and finally the thought of man in his relation to the universe.

Oh, she is coming, the dancer of the future: the free spirit, who will inhabit the body of new woman; more glorious than any woman that has yet been; more beautiful than the Egyptian, than the Greek, the early Italian, than all women of past centuries—the highest intelligence in the freest body!

LIGHT AND THE
DANCE

Loïe Fuller
1862–1928

*L*oïe Fuller, born in Fullersberg, Illinois, was another American
who found a more receptive atmosphere in Europe than in her
native country. After a start in the American theater, she went
abroad. Arriving in Paris in 1892, she was a great success from the
night of her debut at the Folies-Bergère.

The spectacular effect of Fuller's dance resulted from her use of col-
ored theatrical lighting playing on and through the voluminous folds of
silk that were her costume. At the time, light refraction had only begun
to be studied by scientists, and electric stage lighting had just come into
use in the theater. In the other arts, Impressionist painters such as
Claude Monet and Camille Pissarro, and music composers, notably
Claude Debussy, were attempting to capture light refraction in their
works. The artists of Art Nouveau accepted the American dancer as a
revolutionary artist.

Miss Fuller invented many new pieces of theatrical lighting equipment, traveled with a large number of technicians, kept her techniques
a closely guarded secret, and complained of imitators who, she felt,
detracted from her success. She toured widely abroad and in the United
States during her career. Although she turned from solo to group choreography around the turn of the century and founded a school in 1908,
neither her works nor her school lasted. The value of her innovations is
only now receiving recognition.

Loïe Fuller's discovery of the effect of light on cloth is described in
this chapter from her autobiography.

Since it is generally agreed that I have created something new, something composed of light, colour, music, and the dance, more especially of light and the dance, it seems to me that it would perhaps be appropriate, after having considered my creation from the anecdotal and picturesque standpoint, to explain in more serious terms, just what my ideas are relative to my art, and how I conceive it both independently and in its relationship to other arts. If I appear to be too serious I apologise in advance.

I hope that this theoretical "essay" will be better received than a certain practical essay that I undertook, soon after my arrival in Paris, in the cathedral of Notre Dame.

Notre Dame! The great cathedral of which France is justly proud was naturally the objective of one of my earliest artistic pilgrimages, I may say of the very earliest. The tall columns, whose shafts, composed of little assembled columns, rise clear to the vaults; the admirable proportions of the nave; the choir, the seats of old carved oak, and the railings of wrought iron— this harmonious and magnificent pile impressed me deeply. But what enchanted me more than anything else was the marvellous glass of the lateral rose windows, and even more, perhaps, the rays of sunlight that vibrated in the church, in various directions, intensely coloured, as a result of having passed through these sumptuous windows.

I quite forgot where I was. I took my handkerchief from my pocket, a white handkerchief, and I waved it in the beams of coloured light, just as in the evening I waved my silken materials in the rays of my reflectors.

Suddenly a tall imposing man, adorned with a heavy silver chain, which swung from an impressive neck, advanced ceremoniously toward me, seized me by the arm and led me toward the entrance, directing a conversation at me which I appreciated as lacking in friendliness although I did not understand a word. To be brief he dropped me on to the pavement. There he looked at me with so severe an expression that I understood his intention was never to let me enter the church again under any pretext.

My mother was as frightened as I was.

Just then a gentleman came along, who seeing us completely taken aback, asked us what had happened. I pointed to the man with the chain, who was still wrathfully surveying us.

"Ask him about it," I said.

The gentleman translated the beadle's language to me.

"Tell that woman to go away; she is crazy."

Such was my first visit to Notre Dame and the vexatious experience that my love of colour and light caused.

When I came to Europe I had never been inside an art museum. The life that I led in the United States had given me neither motive nor leisure to become interested in masterpieces, and my knowledge of art was hardly worth mentioning. The first museum whose threshold I crossed was the British Museum. Then I visited the National Gallery. Later I became acquainted with the Louvre and, in due course, with most of the great museums of Europe. The circumstance that has struck me most forcibly in regard to these museums is that the architects have not given adequate attention to considerations of light.

Thanks to this defect I get in most museums an impression of a disagreeable medley. When I look at the objects for some moments the sensation of weariness overcomes me, it becomes impossible to separate the things one from another. I have always wondered if a day will not come when this problem of lighting will be better solved. The question of illumination, of reflection, of rays of light falling upon objects, is so essential that I cannot understand why so little importance has been attached to it. Nowhere have I seen a museum where the lighting was perfect. The panes of glass that let the light through ought to be hidden or veiled just as are the lamps that light theatres, then the objects can be observed without the annoyance of the sparkle of the window.

The efforts of the architect ought to be directed altogether in that direction—to the redistribution of light. There are a thousand ways of distributing it. In order that it may fulfill the desired conditions light ought to be brought directly to pictures and statues instead of getting there by chance.

Colour is disintegrated light. The rays of light, disintegrated by vibrations, touch one object and another, and this disintegration, photographed in the retina, is always chemically the result of changes in matter and in beams of light. Each one of these effects is designated under the name of colour.

Our acquaintance with the production and variations of these effects is precisely at the point where music was when there was no music.

In its earliest stage music was only natural harmony; the noise of the waterfall, the rumbling of the storm, the gentle whisper of the west wind, the murmur of the watercourses, the rattling of rain on dry leaves, all the sounds of still water and of the raging sea, the sleeping of lakes, the tumult of the hurricane, the soughing of the wind, the dreadful roar of the cyclone, the crashing of the thunder, the crackling of branches.

Afterwards the singing birds and then all the animals emitted their various sounds. Harmony was there; man, classifying and arranging the sounds, created music.

We all know what man has been able to get from it since then.

Man, past master of the musical realm, is to-day still in the infancy of art, from the standpoint of control of light.

If I have been the first to employ coloured light, I deserve no special praise for that. I cannot explain the circumstance; I do not know how I do it. I can only reply, like Hippocrates when he was asked what time was: "Ask it of me," he said, "and I cannot tell you; ask it not and I know it well."

It is a matter of intuition, of instinct, and nothing else.

Sight is perhaps the first, the most acute, of our senses. But as we are born with this sense sufficiently well developed to enable us to make good use of it, it is afterward the last that we try to perfect. For we concern ourselves with everything sooner than with beauty. So there is no reason for surprise that the colour sense is the last to be developed.

Yet, notwithstanding, colour so pervades everything that the whole universe is busy producing it, everywhere and in everything. It is a continued recurrence, caused by processes of chemical composition and decomposition. The day will come when man will know how to employ them so delightfully that it will be hard to conceive how he could have lived so long in the darkness in which he dwells to-day.

Our knowledge of motion is nearly as primitive as our knowledge of colour. We say "prostrated by grief," but, in reality, we pay attention only to the grief; "transported with joy," but we observe only the joy; "weighed down by chagrin," but we consider only the chagrin. Throughout we place no value on the movement that expresses the thought. We are not taught to do so, and we never think of it.

Who of us has not been pained by a movement of impatience, a lifting of the eyebrows, a shaking of the head, the sudden withdrawal of a hand?

We are far from knowing that there is as much harmony in motion as in music and colour. We do not grasp the facts of motion.

How often we have heard it said: "I cannot bear this colour." But have we ever reflected that a given motion is produced by such and such music? A polka or a waltz to which we listen informs us as to the motions of the dance and blends its variations. A clear sparkling day produces upon us quite a different effect from a dull sad day, and by pushing these observations further we should begin to comprehend some more delicate effects which influence our organism.

In the quiet atmosphere of a conservatory with green glass, our actions are different from those in a compartment with red or blue glass. But usually we pay no attention to this relationship of actions and their causes. These are, however, things that must be observed when one dances to an accompaniment of light and music properly harmonised.

Light, colour, motion, and music.

Observation, intuition, and finally comprehension.

Let us try to forget educational processes in so far as dancing is concerned. Let us free ourselves from the sense that is ordinarily assigned to the word. Let us endeavour to forget what is understood by it today. To rediscover the primitive form of the dance, transformed into a thousand shapes that have only a very distant relationship to it, we shall have to go back to the early history of the race. We then get a notion [of] what the origin of the dance must have been and what has made it what it is to-day.

At present dancing signifies motions of the arms and legs. It means a conventional motion, at first with one arm and one leg, then a repetition of the same figure with the other arm and the other leg. It is accompanied by music, each note calls for a corresponding motion, and the motion, it is unnecessary to say, is regulated rather by the time than by the spirit of the music. So much the worse for the poor mortal who cannot do with his left leg what he does with his right leg. So much [the] worse for the dancer who cannot keep in time, or, to express it better, who cannot make as many motions as there are notes. It is terrifying to consider the strength and ability that are needed for proficiency.

Slow music calls for a slow dance, just as fast music requires a fast dance.

In general, music ought to follow the dance. The best musician is he who can permit the dancer to direct the music instead of the music inspiring the dance. All this is proved to us by the natural outcome of the motives which first impelled men to dance. Nowadays these motives are forgotten, and it is no longer considered that there should be a reason for dancing.

In point of fact the dancer on learning a piece of new music, says: "Oh, I cannot dance to that air." To dance to new music, the dancer has to learn the conventional steps adapted to that music.

Music, however, ought to indicate a form of harmony or an idea with instinctive passion, and this instinct ought to incite the dancer to follow the harmony without special preparation. This is the true dance.

To lead us to grasp the real and most extensive connotation of the word dance, let us try to forget what is implied by the choreographic art of our day.

What is the dance? It is motion.

What is motion? The expression of a sensation.

What is a sensation? The reaction in the human body produced by an impression or an idea perceived by the mind.

A sensation is the reverberation that the body receives when an impression strikes the mind. When the tree bends and resumes its balance it has received an impression from the wind or the storm. When an animal is frightened its body receives an impression of fear, and it flees and trembles or else stands at bay. If it be wounded, it falls. So it is when matter responds to immaterial causes. Man, civilised and sophisticated, is alone best able to inhibit his own impulses.

In the dance, and there ought to be a word better adapted to the thing, the human body should, despite conventional limitations, express all the sensations or emotions that it experiences. The human body is ready to express, and it would express if it were at liberty to do so, all sensations just as the body of an animal.

Ignoring conventions, following only my own instinct, I am able to translate the sensations we have all felt without suspecting that they could be expressed. We all know that in the powerful emotions of joy, sorrow, horror, or despair, the body expresses the emotion it has received from the mind. The mind serves as a medium and causes these sensations to be caught up by the body. In fact, the body responds to these sensations to such an extent sometimes that, especially when the shock is violent, life is suspended or even leaves the body altogether.

But natural and violent movements are possible only in the midst of grand or terrible circumstances. They are only occasional motions.

To impress an idea I endeavour, by my motions, to cause its birth in the spectator's mind, to awaken his imagination, that it may be prepared to receive the image.

Thus we are able, I do not say to understand, but to feel within ourselves as an impulse an indefinable and wavering force, which urges and dominates us. Well, I can express this force which is indefinable but certain in its impact. I have motion. That means that all the elements of nature may be expressed.

Let us take a *"tranche de vie."* That expresses surprise, deception, contentment, uncertainty, resignation, hope, distress, joy, fatigue, feebleness, and, finally, death. Are not all these sensations, each one in turn, humanity's lot? And why can not these things be expressed by the dance, guided intelligently, as well as by life itself? Because each life expresses one by one all these

emotions. One can express even the religious sensations. Can
we not again express the sensations that music arouses in us,
either a nocturne of Chopin's or a sonata of Beethoven's, a slow
movement by Mendelssohn, one of Schumann's lieder, or even
the cadence of lines of poetry?

As a matter of fact, motion has been the starting point of all
effort at self-expression, and it is faithful to nature. In experiencing one sensation we cannot express another by motions,
even when we can do so in words.

Since motion and not language is truthful, we have accordingly perverted our powers of comprehension.

That is what I have wanted to say and I apologise for having said it at such length, but I felt that it was necessary.

THE DANCE AS LIFE EXPERIENCE

Ruth St. Denis
1877–1968

R uth St. Denis found her primary inspiration in the exoticism of the Orient. Dance was very much a spiritual experience for her, at once sensuous and mystical. Born in Somerville, New Jersey, she performed in New York and Europe for a number of years before her marriage to Ted Shawn. Together they established Denishawn, where "Miss Ruth" taught Oriental dance and also choreographed for and performed with the Denishawn company, which toured widely throughout the United States for the next fifteen years. During this period, with the help of Doris Humphrey, she developed "music visualizations."*

Following her separation from Ted Shawn and the dissolution of Denishawn in the early 1930s, St. Denis remained in New York City. There she founded the Society of Spiritual Arts and a Church of Divine Dance, and her rhythmic choir performed in several large churches as well as at the 1939 World's Fair. During World War II, St. Denis returned to Los Angeles, where she worked in an airplane factory for a few months before opening a studio. On her seventieth birthday the Church of Divine Dance was re-founded in Los Angeles. St. Denis remained active in religious dance until shortly before her death.

The following article is taken from Denishawn Magazine, which was published by the school for only two years (1924-1925). A typical issue included essays written by St. Denis and Shawn, as well as poetry by St. Denis.

*Music visualization is the translation of musical structure into movement.

I see men and women dancing rhythmically in joy, on a hilltop bathed in the saffron rays of a setting sun.

I see them moving slowly, with flowing, serene gestures, in the glow of the risen moon. I see them giving praise; praise for the earth and the sky and the sea and the hills, in free, happy movements that are projections of their moods of peace and adoration.

I see the Dance being used as a means of communication between soul and soul—to express what is too deep, too fine for words.

I see children growing straight and proportioned, swift and sure of movement, having dignity and grace and wearing their bodies lightly and with power.

I see our race made finer and quicker to correct itself—because the Dance reveals the soul.

The Dance is motion, which is life, beauty, which is love, proportion, which is power. To dance is to live life in its finer and higher vibrations, to live life harmonized, purified, controlled. To dance is to feel one's self actually a part of the cosmic world, rooted in the inner reality of spiritual being.

The revelation of spiritual beauty in terms of movement is the natural and inevitable progression of life and art; and the word Dancer should rightly mean one who expresses in bodily gesture the joy and power of his being.

Dancing of late years has been degraded to the narrow limits and low level of professionalism—of mere mechanical proficiency, associated always with the most frivolous and ephemeral phases of the stage. But this day is fading. We are slowly advancing beyond this stage of obscuration and perversion. We are turning our gaze inward, learning to seek there the divine sources of the dance, to the end that it may flower into new and more glorious forms of beauty and worth.

We dancers today are struggling and sacrificing and working so that at some precious hour in the future we may live! In truth, we are living now. Behind the veil of our actual, common days is the Eternal Now which is seeking ever to reveal itself—to shed light on the confusion of our heavy hours. But the power of the dance to release the soul is still buried under the weight of the binding and artificial world we have created for ourselves—in which there is no time to know, and no space to move.

The Eternal Now of the Dance includes both past and future. It includes the knowledge and assurance that in the past bodily gesture was the first communication of the simple needs of primitive man, and it includes the vision of the future in which the Cosmic Consciousness, to which man gradually attains, will find expression in finer bodies and more beautiful and articulate gesture.

We can not, of course, communicate, in any language, what we do not feel or know. But in modern times we have used almost exclusively the language of the intellect—speech—to express all states and stages of our consciousness, and by so doing we have inhibited and dwarfed the physical and emotional beauty of the self, while the spiritual consciousness has sought entirely other means for its expression, not knowing that dancing in its nobler uses is the very temple and word of the living spirit.

It is largely from this error that the sense of separation between body and spirit has grown. In reality, each individual self creates and governs its own organ of expression, and with this organ its communication with the world.

Let us, therefore, regard the dance fundamentally as a Life Experience, as the primitive and ultimate means of expression and communication. Let us see in the free, spontaneous dance of every child the beginning of the universal language, and the universal art, which, largely unconscious to himself, grows bodily into words, telling of illusive and exquisite moments of the hidden self; and later flowers into forms of art that will heal the world of some of its artistic sins.

To know this experience, even in a slight degree, to have space and light and music, a real sacrifice is necessary. The physical elements of our present life are designed for other uses, and our days are crowded with profitless confusions. Let there be more beauty and harmonious activity experienced *by* the individual, less merely *for* him. That is the purpose of the Dance. He has too much now of concert, stage, vaudeville and movies.

We are continually urged to go and see this opera or that con-cert—always to be the silent, negative part, providing an audi-ence and support for another's hours of joyous experience. (Let us not forget that the artist's joy is in his work. It is only in the discord of the artist's environment that his suffering lies.)

How much of our precious time is wasted by impositions from without—by having our minds defaced and poisoned by pictures that confuse and weigh down the spirit, in the name of art, because we do not know how to release the divine urge to strength and beauty within ourselves!

Pure dance has no bounds. The infant begins to dance at its mother's knee. Old age should have its gestures to express love and serenity no less. Each period of life has its own activity, its own beauty, and it is stupid and futile to attempt, as we do on the stage in the name of art and entertainment, to force or retard the natural unfolding of the spirit from youth to maturity.

Artificial and limited ideas of the dance have done cruel and grotesque things to its servants, as, indeed, they have to most artists of the stage. The spectacle of a singer or dancer or actor continuing on the stage in parts too young for him is tragic enough—but still more tragic is the situation of the artist who, in his maturity, having grown to the most interesting and beau-tiful stage of his consciousness, is forced to withdraw from his active career because of the childish demand of the public for mere youth. Some day our conceptions will expand to take in, with the loveliness and freshness of childhood, the gracious dignity of age, in art as well as in life. Here the dance will unfold many truths of being, many unknown or unseen joys possible to us in the very midst of our common days.

Make way for the dance! See if it does not repay a thousand fold. It will enlarge the horizon, give meaning to many things now hidden, new power to the self, a new value to existence.

Dancing as a life experience is not something to be taken on from the outside—something to be painfully learned—or something to be imitated.

Dancing is the natural rhythmic movements of the body that have long been suppressed or distorted, and the desire to dance would be as natural as to eat, or to run, or swim, if our civilization had not in countless ways and for divers reasons put its ban upon this instinctive and joyous action of the harmonious being. Our formal religions, our crowded cities, our clothes, and our transportation are largely responsible for the inert mass of humanity that until very lately was encased in collars and corsets. But we are beginning to emerge, to throw off, to demand space to think in and to dance in.

Oh, dancers and lovers of beauty everywhere, come, let us reason together and see if we can not make a better world, "one nearer to our hearts' desire!"

For I see a place of magical Beauty, that is and is not of this world that we know, a world created of familiar things, but arranged in a new and harmonious order.

I see a life lived that bridges the two worlds, the inner and the outer, concept and expression, Nature and Art.

I see groves of meditation, where Truth is learned and loved, and halls of Beauty, where the divine self is expressed.

CONSTANTS—WHAT CONSTITUTES A WORK OF ART IN THE DANCE

Ted Shawn
1891–1972

*T*ed Shawn, the one-time divinity student from Kansas City, Missouri, shared with his wife, Ruth St. Denis, a belief in the validity of dance as religious expression. Many of the dances he choreographed had a religious or ethnic base, and often the two themes were combined. He choreographed, performed, and shared the direction of the Denishawn company and was also responsible for the development of the Denishawn school. His study of Delsarte's theories had a profound effect on him, which carried over into his teaching.

His eclectic approach to dance education was later reflected in the "University of the Dance," which he established at Jacob's Pillow, his summer school of dance in the Berkshire Mountains of western Massachusetts. "The Pillow" continues today, much as he founded it. In the 1930s, after the collapse of Denishawn, he formed Ted Shawn and his Men Dancers, a dance company that toured widely across the country. Although separated, Shawn and St. Denis remained close friends. In 1964 they danced together for the first time in over thirty years, in celebration of their fiftieth wedding anniversary.

Ted Shawn was articulate on the dance and published a number of books. The following essay is taken from a collection of lectures that he delivered at George Peabody College.

Philosophers have tried to tell us that all life is a continuous flux—that nothing is permanent but change. But, somehow, the human soul continually reaches out for something permanent, something enduring. We crave solidity and the eternal in the midst of all evidence that everything is elusive and impermanent. Perhaps it is only wishful thinking on my part, but I believe that this eternal desire of the soul is the greatest argument for the value of "constants" in art. For in art we create our ideal worlds, and in the ideal world of the universal man, there are constant, enduring and never-changing qualities.

In relation to the dance, these constants have two aspects: the physical and the—shall I say?—spiritual (at least spiritual in the sense of art-values).

In the physical realm, the constants are what we, as dancers, must all have and what, critically, we have the right to expect of other dancers. These are bodily skills, mind-body coordinations, disciplines.

No matter what type of dancing is done there are certain things that must be mastered: the dancer must be light, i.e., able to leave the floor by leaping or jumping, and land with elasticity, so as not to jar his body or make a noise. He must have mastered all those fundamental movement patterns which I have elucidated at greater length in my monograph: "The Fundamentals of a Dance Education"—swinging, walking, running, leaping, jumping, falling, torsion, bending, shaking, oppositions, parallelisms, successions, the "alphabet" of those movements out of which dance steps are made; he must be the master of the twin principles of tension and relaxation, and must be able to maintain balance perfectly whether at rest or in motion. He must have his body so trained and so co-ordinated that the idea, be it kinetic, musical or dramatic, is expressed by his whole body as a unity. He must know thoroughly the patterns of construction of dance in relation to all three dimensions of space, and in relation to that fourth dimension of the dance: time. He must be trained in the relation of the dance to music so that, when dancing to music, his movement and the music seem the twin emanation of one impulse, and he must master the relationship of himself to a group of other dancers in an almost infinite variety of patterns. In addition to this he must apprehend all the different *qualities* of movement, and be able to produce these qualities as surely as the organist pulls out the stops on his organ. He must acquire a rich vocabulary of movements, so that he can improvise as easily as he indulges in a pleasant and exciting conversation, never stopping to think what word to use, nor how to form his sentence grammatically. And he must have acquired and mastered a technique (many techniques, really) or else build a technique for himself, by doing which he has administered to himself a more severe discipline than if he had been trained in the technique of others.

These, then, are constants—we must deal with all of these if we expect to dance ourselves, and we have a right to expect these in dancers we see, and fairly judge the value and quality of the performance by the degree the dancer shows us how he has absorbed, mastered and practically forgotten these constants.

But beyond these physical constants there are the greater constants. For no matter how cleverly a dancer dances, no matter how disciplined and technically proficient he be—if the dance he performs is inexpertly constructed, and the content worthless or thin, we are disappointed and "let down."

These greater constants are those which we look for in the dance itself—the dance as a work of art—where we are judging the work of the composer, the author, that is, the choreographer.

In actual physical performance, the dance has many unique problems which are not shared by any other art form, but the standards by which we judge a dance as a work of art (the dance in itself, as distinct from the performance of it) are almost the identical standards by which we judge a work of art in any other medium.

First, there should be complete clarity in the mind of the creator as to what he intends to do (that is, to say, in his own particular medium of the dance). He may wish to create a mood, or he may wish to tell a story, or he may wish only to take a "seed" of basic movement, and let it be organically developed into a final complicated-yet-simple product. Whatever his aim, the choreographer must not be confused as to his intention, his method, his stylization, the special technique used, or the result will be hybrid, confusing, neither one thing nor the other.

Second, there must be unity of style in the composition, one quality of movement must remain throughout. This does not mean that there can be no variety, but that the variety must be within the unity. The work as a whole must be of one stuff, as an emerald is all emerald—crush it to powder, and each tiny pinch of that powder will still be emerald. A fragment of a Greek vase is instantly recognizable, and each fragment of any dance which is a work of art should be sufficiently stylized to identify the whole from which it was taken. And, within this unity, the work must cohere—it must be solid in its construction, so that there are no joining places left visible in the finished product—but it seems to have been quarried out of one piece.

This means that the dance must have sequence, each movement done must lead inevitably into the next movement, so that one could not imagine any other movement being possible as successor to the movement just done.

And this implies, absolutely, architecture. The whole dance, as a work of art, must be constructed as well and carefully as a beautiful building, which is beautiful not only because of its materials and ornamentation, but also on account of its design, its proportions; because it has a solid foundation, and because its walls are solid and capable of supporting the roof. A dance work of art must have beginning, development and climax—just as a building has foundations, walls and roof.

Since the dance is almost universally accompanied by music, there are certain constants in that relationship, too. The dance must have in it all the qualities that the music has and provide, in replica, all the elements of the music. Of course, the foundation is rhythm—the without-which-nothing—the thing on which all rests. But, as music has harmony so must the movement be harmonious within itself and with the music. Even if one is dancing to the apparent dissonances of modern music, there must be a harmony between the distortion—consciously and intelligently used—of the body and the distortions of tone from the accepted norm. All the values of time, duration, stress, dynamics and form inherent in the music, must be equally inherent in the dance work of art.

Much has been and still is said about kinesthesia, about dance being kinetically created, but this is one only of the legitimate starting points for the creation of a dance, and it never excuses formlessness in the finished product. Many things that are permissible in the studio as training, as experimentation, as discipline, are not permissible to offer to an audience as a dance work of art. Many people who are interested in the dance may enjoy visiting a class and watching the training process, but studio exercises should be confined to the studio, and never be brought to an exhibition program of the supposedly finished, product.

We hear the word "stylized" a great deal in regard to the dance. This refers to what I said about unity. A dancer may choose to do a dance in the style of the hieratic wall paintings of ancient Crete, or in the style of a Javanese dance, or a Spanish dance. In this case, this style must predominate, govern and discipline every movement, and even the dance as a whole. The dancer may develop such a strong individual style that his movement may be "stylized" and yet not be classifiable as belonging to any actual style such as those mentioned above; yet within his own style he maintains a unity of quality and is disciplined by his own imposed limitations.

"Distortion" is another word much discussed in the dance today. From a certain angle, all art is distortion, in that it is not a photographic, mechanical reproduction of nature. The artist chooses from out of the vast superfluity of nature that which he wishes to use, shapes that to his own purpose, and so "distorts" it from its original form and shape. But "distortion" is a dangerous word, for many people seem to think that wrenching things blindly into grotesque shapes has value in itself. Those who have revolted unintelligently from the ballet tradition and technique seem to believe that the exact opposite of the rules of the ballet will give some strangely desirable result. This produces movement without real significance—or perhaps it has some significance: that of the naughty child who makes faces to show that it doesn't like a person.

Do not be afraid that, because you are teachers, and especially teachers in Physical Education, that all this talk about "art" is beside the point. It is very definitely to the point, because the dance is art, or it is nothing. It is not merely a means of exercising, or promoting health, or building a strong symmetrical body. It does all these things, and better than any other means of physical education, but these are all by-products. An art activity is the deepest, richest, most worth-while activity of mankind. It is work and it is play—the most delightful play ever known, and "that work most worthy of man's perfected powers." We must be conscious of the dance as art even when we are teaching the simplest beginning fundamentals, and try to awaken that attitude towards the dance in all our pupils. The value of the dance, its greatest value, is in the "intangibles." Success in the dance cannot be measured by a tape, weighed on scales, nor timed with a stop-watch. It demands an awareness and sensitivity in the dancer's soul and in the soul of the beholder who partakes vicariously, empathetically, in the dance—and it is the development, strengthening and cultivation of this awareness which is the teacher's most important job.

You must clear your mind of all misconceptions of what art means—get out of your head, if possible and if you have any of that feeling there, that art is something in museums, something remote and precious. Art is experience, vital experience, and nowhere does one experience the reality of art so greatly as in the dance. Here the constants of beauty, ease, proportion, vitality, technical mastery, of the communication of ecstasy to the beholder, are within one's body-soul—they are as much you as your blood and your breath. And the greatest constant of all is that here in the dance we experience a rhythmic beauty, the activity of God Himself.

STAGE DANCE—
STAGE DANCER

Mary Wigman
1886–1973

Mary Wigman, a native of Germany and a student of Dalcroze and Laban, developed a new dance form that has often been called "absolute dance." It was a unique combination of her training, her personality, her Germanic heritage, and the atmosphere of pre-Nazi Europe. Often expressionistic, it was similar to the work of German Expressionist painters, notably Emil Nolde, who had a direct influence on Wigman. Her works ranged from gentle dances of nature to the macabre. She believed that "art grows out of the basic cause of existence."

Wigman was the leading force in German modern dance for some fifty years. Her school, founded in Dresden in 1920, developed branches all over Germany, and also one in New York. During World War II she lived in Leipzig, where she taught only a small number of students, but in 1949 she reestablished her school in West Berlin and continued to teach until blindness and old age forced her to retire in the late 1960s.

The essay reprinted here was originally written in 1927, yet Wigman's ideas have the ring of timeless truths.

We find ourselves in a process of change as far as the dance is concerned: abandonment of the classical ballet in favor of an expression representing our time. On the one hand, it would indicate a deterioration of the classical ballet and the traditional corps de ballet at the opera houses. On the other hand, the advance of a few personalities in the dance field to whom the

ballet denied the expression of their creative ideas because of its set vocabulary and style.

What are we looking for? To attune our inmost feelings to the mood of our time. Everywhere appear solo dancers and dance groups. A wild mixture of good and bad accomplishments, bold attempts, and daring experiments results in apparent confusion—a condition which, on second thought, is quite natural. Can we expect from this hardly twenty-year-old child of our time that it should have its own tradition by now? Even if one invokes the usual slogan about the speed of our time, one cannot demand the impossible.

Our dance would be of little meaning and would have no life nor enduring quality at all had we already conquered it to such an extent that its possibilities were clearly defined, its style set, and its development decided upon. We had better be patient and wait until the unorganic parts get lost and the pure fulfilled form becomes crystallized. It cannot be denied that our body awareness was unknown to any former generation the way it is now. Interest in physical movement, from all kinds of sports to artistic dancing, is now alive and will remain so. The strengthening and ennobling of the body as well as body expression have become slogans which may make sense but can only turn into fulfillment generations later. Genuine accomplishments need time to mature even in our fast-paced life.

The confusion in the field of movement is great and yet not so great as it may appear to the uninitiated. There may be many systems and methods of gymnastics, but they all point to one purpose: to control the body for the body's sake. The ultimate and noblest meaning of the dance can have one aim only: the living work of art presented through the human body as its instrument of expression. The manifoldness of dance expression was overwhelming and confusing after its divorce from the set world of the classical ballet. Gradually, the dance scene can more easily be surveyed. Even the skeptic will have to admit that the so-called "modern" dance has gained a great deal of ground in the short time of its existence, and not only in its own artistic right, but also in its effect on all other art forms.

Two essential types of creative dancing are the *absolute* dance and the *stage* dance. A parallel can be found in music. The absolute dance is independent of any literary-interpretative content; it does not represent, it is; and its effect on the spectator who is invited to experience the dancer's experience is on a mental-motoric level, exciting and moving. If it still happens that we see in absolute dancing any definable action in a theatrical sense, then the fault lies only partly with the dance creation. The difficulty usually lies with the spectator, who has not yet learned to absorb dance as pure dance without seeing in it some perceived or imagined imagery. The stage dance works with the same means as the absolute dance, but it is predetermined by the "scenic" event. The decorative element is evoked by set, lighting, and costume. The main accent is no longer on the dance itself but on the total stage event.

Pantomime is one of the purest forms of the stage dance when it interprets meaningful action by means of mere dancing. The actor's pantomimic gesture has been completely absorbed by the [silent] film. What music is to the opera, pantomime is to dance. Pantomime need not be limited to the old-fashioned shepherd's plays or idylls and harlequinades; all doors are open to pantomime in whatever can be represented by means of the dance, from symbolic events to the most realistic happenings.

It has been said that the stage dance has not stood the test and the dancers proved a failure. This may be true in certain cases, but cannot be applied to all contemporary dance accomplishments. I would like to shed light on this situation in showing how it looks to me. Not only is the modern dance too young to be up to all the requirements imposed upon it, nor is the dancer sufficiently mature to fulfill all the demands asked of him. There are very few stages in Germany that have a homogeneous dance group trained in the modern dance idiom. In most cases the young dancers become a part of an established classical ballet ensemble. And these ballet groups are not only differently trained, they are no longer able to do justice to the spirit of our time. The artistic results of such a dance group, diversely oriented, cannot be satisfactory, at least not overnight. More often than not, well-meant attempts are doomed to failure. In most cases a compromise is found between the two techniques, and "modern" is being danced today, then again "classic" tomorrow, without adhering to the one or the other.

Hardly anyone of the gifted young people turning to the dance wants to become a ballet dancer—at least, at the moment here in Germany. They all want to dance the way they feel, and the dancer's sensibility is rather uniform and directed toward expressing the spirit of today's generation, however inadequate his artistic expression may be. Today's dancers—who, in contrast to former times, do not exclusively belong to a certain stratum of society but come from all walks of life—expect more from the dance as a profession than to make a living. They see in the dance a possibility to express their very being, they envision the stage as a place of artistic creation where they can develop their abilities and fight for new ideas. It is no longer enough for our youth—regardless of how far advanced he is as [a] dancer—to take part in the ballet episode of an opera, to hop around in a peasant *Reigen,* or to cross the stage in the role of a page carrying an orb made of papier-mâché. He asks for more and has a right to do so. He asks for tasks for which it pays to work and struggle, and it often enough happens that, after a short while, he loses interest and tires of the little ability he has acquired.

We certainly do not find the same condition everywhere, and there are theatres in Germany where the dance gets full attention and the dancer is able to prove himself. But it also happens that after acceptance of the first bold attempts, the interest of the public and press in the new dance group wanes, and sometimes also a sudden disinterest in the theatre administration makes things difficult for the dancers. One loses patience when the young and motley ensemble does not achieve a uniform capacity within one season, or when the choreographer does not display a stunning dance idea each month. From where should they all come, the perfectly trained dancers with masterly accomplishments, the unusually gifted balletmasters and choreographers and dance composers? They do not have the time to develop and to prepare themselves, inwardly and outwardly, for the responsibility of their profession.

We must not overlook that our time is characterized not only by many positive as well as negative accomplishments, but also by a serious economic crisis. Who, nowadays, can still afford to finish any of his studies? The young dancers are—like any other working people—the bearers and victims of our time. Almost without exception, after one or two years of study they must make a living. How can they accomplish anything close to perfection under such conditions? They need the theatre not only as a place to work in, but also for their extended study. Above all, they need a guiding spirit in the theatre whom they can trust and who would undertake to further their study. But this balletmaster, who ought to be a choreographer and, if possible, a composer at the same time (for there are no ready-made modern dance works which can be rehearsed and performed) usually comes to his position under similar circumstances. He too has not enough experience and an insufficient storehouse of imagination to enable him to stage one work after the other.

It may be well to compare the developing career of a conductor with that of a modern choreographer. In his studies during many years at a conservatory and at colleges the conductor must first prove that he really is a "musician." He must master the piano and know the other instruments, he must be able to read a score, must be familiar with all styles of music from the classic to the avant-garde composers. If, after the completion of his studies, he succeeds in obtaining a post at a theatre, he does not start in a leading position and is not immediately charged with difficult tasks. He first acts as a coach and assistant to the chief conductor of the house. He thus starts the second half of his studies and knows that it may take a couple of years before he will lead the orchestra. In case he proves to be a strong talent, a musician and conductor of some merit, he will undoubtedly be noticed and his ability will become known despite all the difficulties which any ambitious young talent must face in a theatre following traditional concepts. Such an intermediate period is nonexistent for the choreographer. After much too little study and without any practical experience in the theatre, he takes over a position which is just as responsible as the one of a conductor.

My personal experiences have made it clear to me how difficult it is to train and develop a dance talent and to integrate it into a dance ensemble. It cannot be pasted on from the outside, it only comes about within a spirited, ideal workshop. Every young person has a strong feeling for a common cause, and, when handled with understanding, the individual will and desire for self-expression will never come in conflict with the teamwork. The necessary raising of the individual and total accomplishments is possible only if one can muster the patience to protect and further each individual talent within the team, to utilize the given abilities creatively within the framework of the projected dance itself.

The concert stage where the modern dancer first maintained himself, with the theatres not yet open to him, could be taken as a criterion for his accomplishments, as the touchstone for his potentialities. However, it presupposes a certain maturity not only of the dancer, but also of the public invited to share the dancer's experience and to criticise him. And it must be said once and for all that the public has to take its share of blame for innumerable incompetent dance performances. As long as it will remain in the habit of applauding a few nice legs of girls who, with their best intentions, stamp their rhythms, as long as mere ambition and misunderstood individual pride can present themselves under the guise of dance, neither will the chaos in the field be set right nor will the level be lifted. We must reach the point where, above and beyond everything else, the dance is evaluated as a work of art and the dancer as the interpreter of an art form, as is done in all other arts. But we must also learn to discriminate between the gratification of personal vanity and a young talent testing its mettle for the first time. The right to appear in public may be a question of talent and creative ability, but even more so of personality, of the stage magnetism which one cannot teach nor learn.

By no means do I want to create the impression that I wish to apologize for dance and dancer with these words, or protect mediocre and bad artistry. I think I have sufficiently proved through my own work as a dancer and choreographer that the

demands imposed on myself and my students are not small and
have contributed to a higher level of dance creation in many
ways. But for the sake of a better future development of the
dance I deemed it necessary to approach the dancers with my
thoughts about them and their craft and also to do justice to
the situation in which they find themselves today. Our dance is
born of our age and its spirit, it has the stamp of our time as no
other art form has. I wish that our contemporaries would
become fully aware of their responsibilities toward their own
and most alive creation, the modern dance. It does not suffice
to support occasional feats of accomplishment. They ought to
prepare with the dancer the ground for the unfolding of the
art's future.

Part Two

THE FOUR
PIONEERS

INTRODUCTION

Called at various times "Papa Shawn" and the "Father of American Dance," Ted Shawn was the kind of parent who required submission and inspired rebellion in his offspring. The first of the famous Denishawn "children" to leave the fold was Martha Graham in 1923. Although Shawn had been her primary teacher and had featured her in his dances, she felt that she must strike out on her own.

The next defectors from Denishawn left in a group in 1928, joining forces for the next sixteen years. Doris Humphrey, star performer and main teacher in the Denishawn school; Charles Weidman, also a performer and teacher there; and Pauline Lawrence, school accompanist, together established the Humphrey-Weidman Dance Company in New York City. These "unholy three" were voted out of Denishawn for disloyalty when Humphrey and Weidman refused to give up their experiments with movement to tour with the Ziegfield Follies. The tour was to raise money for "Greater Denishawn," at that point, a huge, unpaid-for house in the suburbs of New York City.

Shortly before that confrontation, Humphrey had been chided by Shawn for not teaching straight Denishawn technique in classes. Instead, she had been testing the discoveries she was beginning to make about dance movement.

Paramount among these, and the basis for the technique she was to develop, was her concept that dance takes place in an arc of unbalance, that is the motion which occurs between the vertical (standing) and the horizontal (lying down) positions. This is the basis of the Humphrey Fall and Recovery Theory.

Martha Graham had also begun to develop a new dance technique which continued to evolve out of her choreography during her entire career. The style which she developed was sharp, angular, and percussive; the most distinctive movement, in her technique, the contraction and release involving the torso, resulted from her observations of breathing.

This was the beginning of American modern dance. For the first time American dancers were creating new movements for new subject matter, and reflecting their own era rather than a previous one. Their movements evolved from the meaning of the dance, rather than from previously learned steps developed by peoples of a different culture. In the process of finding new techniques to express their art, these modern dance pioneers broke the existing rules; indeed, that was their intent, for they were anti-Denishawn, anti-ballet, anti-the past.

The percussive, angular, and often distorted movements of early modern dance expressed the tensions of contemporary life. Similar developments in other arts resulted in the Cubist paintings of Picasso and Braque and the dissonant music of Hindemith and Schoenberg. At the same time, dance ceased to be regarded primarily as entertainment, and through the new aesthetics, it achieved the status of a serious, creative, independent art form.

All levels of the dancers' space were used, resulting in a relationship to gravity that was in direct contrast to the *danse verticale* of the Romantic ballet. The torso became fully active as it was freed of its balletic rigidity, and the dancers angled their limbs, in contrast to the extended line of ballet. Interestingly, many of these movements can be traced to the Denishawn origins of the pioneers, particularly to the Oriental and Delsartean influences. The difference between the old and the new was that these modern dance originators used the principles they had learned from Denishawn to create new movements. Their first dances accordingly showed a lingering Denishawn influence, but in time they worked away from it, although their warm-up exercises continued to include a combination of yoga and ballet.

The dancers' costumes and stage settings were extremely simplified, often to the point of starkness. The dance itself was performed either to music written for it by a contemporary composer or to no music at all; occasionally, music of the pre-classic or classic period was used. The dancers performed wherever they could: in lofts, studios, and small theaters in New York

City, and in colleges and university auditoriums and gymnasiums throughout the country.

Critics played an important role in bringing this avant-garde movement before the public eye and in expanding its small but devoted following. John Martin, a staff critic for *The New York Times* from 1927 to 1962, had a background in theater but soon began covering modern dance performances extensively, becoming the foremost champion of the fledgling art and the first "dean" of dance critics.

By the time that Louis Horst founded *Dance Observer* in 1934, he was already an old friend of the modern dancers. As a musician he had accompanied classes and performances at Denishawn. He left in 1925, becoming Martha Graham's advisor, critic, and music composer. In addition, he developed a formal approach to the teaching of dance composition, which has been experienced by countless students over the years. This approach uses art forms and styles from all periods of human history except that in which ballet developed. *Dance Observer* presented reviews, articles, and advertisements devoted principally to modern dance, and Horst continued monthly publication until his death in 1964.

Walter Terry, who studied with Shawn, Graham, Humphrey, Limón, and others, was another critic who supported modern dance through his reviews in the *New York Herald-Tribune*. Martin, Horst, and Terry have all written definitive books on dance.

In 1931 Hanya Holm came from Germany to open the New York branch of the Mary Wigman School. She had studied with Dalcroze, Laban, and Wigman before becoming a Wigman company member and teacher. By 1936 she had established the Hanya Holm School and Company, and the New York Wigman School was dissolved. German modern dance, which up to this time had developed parallel to American modern dance, was thus injected into the mainstream of American modern dance. This dance form, characterized by its use of space and of improvisation as a teaching tool, has retained its uniqueness through the followers of the Laban-Wigman-Holm tradition in this country.

Modern dance coalesced as a movement through the efforts of two far-sighted young women, Martha Hill and Mary Jo Shelly, who established the Bennington College School of the Dance in 1934. There they invited the leading modern dancers to teach and create. Martha Graham, Doris Humphrey, Charles Weidman, and Hanya Holm were the permanent faculty from 1934 until its closing in 1941.

The economic stability, the artistic freedom, the space, and the chance to perform gave these four pioneers the opportunity to focus their energies on the creation of larger works during the summer months. Some of these works composed and presented there remain as milestones of modern dance, such as *Deaths and Entrances* and *Letter to the World* by Martha Graham, *With My Red Fires* and *Passacaglia and Fugue in C Minor* by Doris Humphrey, and *Trend* by Hanya Holm.

World War II began a period of disruption in the careers of the pioneers. The Bennington School of the Dance closed; male dancers were drafted into the armed forces; tours of the "gymnasium circuit" of colleges and universities, long a financial mainstay of modern dance companies, declined. Financial difficulties forced the disbandment of the Hanya Holm Company in 1944. Miss Holm turned to choreography for Broadway musicals while continuing to teach at her New York studio and at the Colorado College summer sessions.

Nineteen forty-four also saw the end of Doris Humphrey's performing career, owing to an arthritic hip. For a brief time she considered total retirement. But then she found a vehicle for her creativity in José Limón, a former member of her company who had just been released from the U.S. Army. She became artistic director for his company and composed some of her best-known works for it. She also continued to teach choreography.

Following the breakup of his partnership with Doris Humphrey in 1945, Charles Weidman continued to teach, choreograph, and maintain a company and studio theater. Because he had depended heavily on her, he found it difficult going alone as his financial problems grew. However, in spite of the drawbacks, he was able to choreograph a number of important works in the years that followed.

Of the original four pioneers, only Martha Graham was still in full command of her performing powers at the end of World War II. And the peak of her creative career was still ahead of her.

Two other important dancers of this generation were Helen Tamiris and Lester Horton.

Helen Tamiris combined ballet and Delsartean theory learned from Irene Lewisohn to create her own style of modern dance. In 1930 she attempted to unify modern dancers through the cooperative performances of the Dance Repertory Theater, but unification was not to be realized. Together with her husband, Daniel Nagrin, she founded the Tamiris-Nagrin Company in 1960, which was dissolved with her death in 1966.

Influenced by Denishawn, Mary Wigman, the Japanese dancer Michio Ito, American Indians, and ballet, Lester Horton organized a dance company in Los Angeles in 1932, which was notable as the first company to include African-Americans. Although he was aware of the activities of the modern dancers in New York, he preferred to work in isolation from them. Following his untimely death in 1953, some of the dancers from his company continued their own careers, including Alvin Ailey, Carmen de Lavallade, Bella Lewitzky, Joyce Trisler, and James Truitte. Through these dancers Horton's eclectic, individualistic technique and choreography were kept alive.

GRAHAM 1937

Martha Graham
1894–1991

*B*orn near Pittsburgh, Pennsylvania, and raised in Santa Barbara California, Martha Graham, like Isadora Duncan, Ruth St. Denis, and Doris Humphrey, had a remarkably strong mother who encouraged her. She began her early days of dance as a student and performer at Denishawn, where she worked principally with Ted Shawn. She made her debut there in 1916 and remained until 1923.

Graham's first independent concert, given in New York City in 1926, had eighteen dances on the program, performed by three other women and her. Throughout her evolving periods and styles, strong, dynamic women of history and literature provided the inspiration for many of the roles she created for herself in her works.

The Martha Graham School of Contemporary Dance was founded in New York in 1927. The dance technique that is still taught there developed out of movements Graham created for her choreography. As her technique was taught and retaught by many other dancers, it became codified and systematized.

The long span of Graham's career contributed to and set the pace for the establishment of modern dance as a valid, independent art form, and her company has provided the starting point for many of the major choreographers who have followed her. After her retirement as a performer in 1969, Graham continued to direct and choreograph for her company. In 1976 she celebrated her company's fiftieth anniversary with a gala performance and the premiere of Lucifer, performed by Margot Fonteyn and Rudolf Nureyev. She created the popular and humorous Maple Leaf Rag to the music of Scott Joplin in 1990, and was working on a new work for the Olympics at the time of her death.

Graham's philosophical outlook, as expressed in this essay, remained unchanged throughout her career.

Throughout time dance has not changed in one essential function. The function of the dance is communication. The responsibility that dance fulfill its function belongs to us who are dancing today.

To understand dance for what it is, it is necessary we know from whence it comes and where it goes. It comes from the depths of man's inner nature, the unconscious, where memory dwells. As such it inhabits the dancer. It goes into the experience of man, the spectator, awakening similar memories.

Art is the evocation of man's inner nature. Through art, which finds its roots in man's unconscious—race memory—is the history and psyche of race brought into focus.

We are making a transition from 18th to 20th century thinking. A new vitality is possessing us. Certain depths of the intellect are being explored. Great art never ignores human values. Therein lies its roots. This is why forms change.

No art can live and pass untouched through such a vital period as we are now experiencing. Man is discovering himself as a world.

All action springs from necessity. This necessity is called by various names: inspiration, motivation, vision, genius. There is a difference of inspiration in the dance today.

Once we strove to imitate gods—we did god dances. Then we strove to become part of nature by representing natural forces in dance forms—winds—flowers—trees.

Dance was no longer performing its function of communication. By communication is not meant to tell a story or to project an idea, but to communicate experience by means of action and perceived by action. We were not speaking to that insight in man which would elevate him to a new strength through a heightened sense of awareness. Change had already taken place in man, was already in his life manifestations. While the arts do not create change, they register change.

This is the reason for the appearance of the modern dance.

The departure of the dance from classical and romantic delin-
eations was not an end in itself, but the means to an end. It was
not done perversely to dramatize ugliness, or to strike at sacred
tradition—to destroy from sheer inability to become proficient
in the technical demands of a classical art. The old forms could
not give voice to the more fully awakened man. They had to
undergo metamorphosis—in some cases destruction—to serve
as a medium for a time differently organized.

The modern dance, as we know it today, came after the
World War. This period following the war demanded forms
vital enough for the reborn man to inhabit. Because of the
revitalized consciousness came an alteration in movement—the
medium of dance, as tone is medium. Out of this came a different use of the body as an instrument, as the violin is an
instrument. Body is the basic instrument, intuitive, instinctive.
As a result an entirely contemporary set of technics was
evolved. While it had points of similarity with the old, that was
because it was based on the innate co-ordination of the body
which is timeless. With this enhanced language, and the more
vitally organized instrument, the body, we are prepared for a
deep, stirring creative communication.

All of this has nothing to do with propaganda as known and
practiced. It only demands the dance be a moment of passionate, completely disciplined action, that it communicate participation to the nerves, the skin, the structure of the spectator.

For this to be accomplished, however, it means that the communication be valid to the twentieth century man. There has
been swift transition in this present recurrence of the modern
dance. There was a revolt against the ornamented forms of
impressionistic dancing. There came a period of great austeri-
ty. Movement was used carefully and significantly. Subject matter began to diverge—the dancer emerged from the realm of
introspection. The dance began to record evolution in man's
thinking. An impassioned dynamic technic was needed and
gradually appeared. Dance accompaniment and costume were
stripped to essentials. Music came to be written on the dance
structure. It ceased to be the source of the emotional stimulus
and was used as background. Music was used almost in the

same sense that decor had been used in the older dance to bring the emotional content of the movement into focus for the spectator. As dance evolved into larger forms, music began to evolve also. The composer gained a greater strength and a more significant line from composing to meet the passionate requirements of the dance.

Then arose a danger. With music no longer acting in that capacity, what means to employ for focus—a focus suited to the eyes of today? Dance can remain for a time an authentic, creative experience for the comparative few. There are those for whom focus is possible—because of their awareness and their response to the artist and his medium. But for the many the focus is not sharp enough to permit clear vision. At this point the responsibility rests with the dancer-choreographer. Now it seems necessary that the focus be made through sight.

While music for the dance is still transparent and exciting as an element, we still use the perennial black velvet curtain of another period as background. They were first used for the dance I believe by Isadora Duncan. She used them, from the same need we have today, to bring focus upon the dance, and she succeeded. But the dance today is another dance, brought into emergence by another orientation. Perhaps what Arch Lauterer calls "space man" will be as necessary to the dance of the future as the composer. All of life today is concerned with space problems, even political life. Space language is a language we understand. We receive so much of sensation through the eye.

It is understood without question that presentation can never take the place of the dance. It can only cover bad and unauthentic dancing as music was long able to do. But this evolved presentation will have nothing to do with dance decor in the older sense, which was basically a painting enlarged for the stage. At best it can only be an accent for the dance, evolved after the dance is finished. Dance decor can, I believe, serve as a means of enhancing movement and gesture to the point of revelation of content.

I refuse to admit that the dance has limitations that prevent its acceptance and understanding—or that the intrinsic purity of the art itself need be touched. The reality of the dance is its truth to our inner life. Therein lies its power to move and communicate experience. The reality of dance can be brought into focus—that is into the realm of human values—by simple, direct, objective means. We are a visually stimulated world today. The eye is not to be denied. Dance need not change—it has only to stand revealed.

WHAT A DANCER THINKS ABOUT

Doris Humphrey
1895–1958

*W*hen Doris Humphrey reached Denishawn from her hometown of Oak Park, Illinois, in 1915, she had already had many years of dance study as well as some teaching experience. She soon became a teacher at the Denishawn school and a leading performer with the company. In addition to assisting Ruth St. Denis with choreography, she created dances of her own, which became part of the Denishawn repertoire.

By the time Doris Humphrey left Denishawn in 1928, she had begun choreographing in a totally new style, and she had developed a fundamental theory of movement that became the basis of her technique. Together with Charles Weidman, who left Denishawn at the same time, Humphrey founded the Humphrey-Weidman Dance Company, based in New York. Both partners taught, choreographed, and performed together in each other's works for the next sixteen years. When the Humphrey-Weidman Company was disbanded in 1945, she became the artistic director of the company of José Limón and continued to display her ability as a master choreographer with a mature sense of artistry. Always articulate, she set forth her choreographic principles in The Art of Making Dances, *which was published shortly after her death.*

The following essay, written about 1937 as the first chapter of a book that was never completed, describes an insider's view of dance.

THE DANCER ANSWERS SOME QUESTIONS

On reflecting about a long career in the theatre as a dancer, I recall numerous people who have offered me questions and remarks, usually in a pressing crowd backstage after a performance. Since I had no time to answer them properly then, my conscience, or is it my egotism, prompts me to send the answers out into space, hoping that the woman in Oklahoma who liked it but didn't know why, and the student in California who thought it must be good exercise, but "what is it all about?" will chance to read this book and be wiser. These people, who are fairly numerous, must be the visible seventh of an iceberg that reaches into the cold, dark depths of America, and it is my hope that some of these may be thawed out too. In case I should seem, in the following pages, to be pouncing too much on the least intelligent members of our audience, may I say that there are hundreds of people who have been most appreciative, and who have said just the right things to warm the heart of any creative artist. My intention, however, is to crusade and not to eulogize; hence the attack on the misunderstanding that exists about the Modern Dance in the mind of that most important person in the theatre—the ultimate consumer.

One of the things often said to me in a backstage crush is: "You must be glad you took up dancing. It's such nice work. But don't you get awfully tired? You do three or four hours [of] rehearsal, besides the performance. My! I'd be dead, but I suppose you like it and it *is* nice work." One of these speeches has the effect of paralyzing me, and a feeble "yes" is about all I can manage at the time. The implications are so staggering that it certainly will take many words to try to strip off the layers and layers of asbestos wrappings overlaying the true responsiveness to the dance which I firmly believe everyone possesses. "Taking up dancing" perhaps enrages me most as a phrase. Dancing, by implication, is a hobby which one "takes up," like gardening or rug weaving, and what makes it "nice work" is that people will pay to see it or learn it. It obviously makes you tired sometimes, and this confuses our poor stupid one. Why work to the point of exhaustion? That can't be much fun. This is, no doubt, put

down to the inexplicable vagaries of artists, who are notori-
ously lacking in common sense. They just let their enthusiasms
run away with them. Once a man told me that, during a long
passage when I was lying on the floor in one of my dances, all
he could think of was rushing up on the stage with a blanket.
The dramatic scene that was going on at the same time passed
him by because he could not forget that females do not lie partially nude on cold floors. It isn't sensible to pursue even nice
work that far.

The next remark of my original questioner, that "I'd be dead
doing that," reveals another terrific gap in her perceptions (usually it's a woman; no man of the same calibre would imagine
doing it at all). The highly trained body of the dancer is as different from that of the non-dancer as an antelope from an ox.
They both breathe and move their legs and have similar nervous systems so they both belong to the animal kingdom, but
the ox is a handsome, dignified, and integrated creature the way
he is and wouldn't dream of overstepping the limitations of his
species or care to embarrass the antelope with suggestions as to
how *he* would look bounding from crag to crag like that.
Parenthetically, however, the similarities in physical construction and function between our two kinds of human animals are
quite sufficient to make the layman understand the dancer,
given a direct and simple approach, with no nonsense about the
dancer's function being a kind of glorified fancy-work. Of this,
much more later.

I should like our audiences to know: first—that one does not
"take up dancing" in my kind of theatre, any more than Aimee
McPherson took up evangelism, or Geraldine Farrar singing.
The dancer is born with, or cultivates an overwhelming desire
to dance, and to communicate his findings about life in this
medium. No, he doesn't think of dancing as "nice work," or as
a way to make a living, but as an imperative urge, a call. He
wants to make his art mean something to people, not superfi-
cially as entertainment, but to their real selves, the selves they
bring to living and that they sometimes bring to be fed at the
springs of the other arts, notably music and literature. In other
words, he wants to make it significant.

SIGNIFICANCE IN THE DANCE VERSUS LITERATURE

Significance can hardly be justified in the eyes of non-dancers
without some explanation. They may ask, and often do: "Why
make the Dance significant, when there is already at hand such
a completely expressive medium as literature? I think dancing
should be graceful." The thought of significant dancing per-
plexes the modern mind, which is trained to slide easily from
idea to expression only in well-greased literary channels. In
fact, the idea of art, with the exception of literature, conveying
anything other than simple conceptions of the beautiful, is
quite unfamiliar. People on the whole are slaves of "The Word"
and the tendency is to believe that if it cannot be written it
cannot be said at all, or even that it does not exist. As an
extreme instance of this: I once knew a man who did not learn
to write until he was twenty-five years old. When he did, however, the revelation of "The Word" took tremendous hold on
him. In his idle moments he would write his name on a scrap
of paper, and gaze at the miracle of it for fifteen minutes. "The
Word" made him an entity. It confirmed an existence of which
he had entertained some doubt until he learned to write it
down. He typifies the prejudice of our times towards the exclusive expression of the Self through the medium of words,
which certainly are indispensable for the ordering of groceries,
or the writing of a treatise on political economy, but in my
opinion are by no means able to express the whole man. "The
Word" is easier for man. It comprehends his daily living, but at
the same time its limitations restrict his cultural life. The simplest mind unconsciously admits that it is not enough to be
able to speak. How often do we hear such a phrase as: "Words
cannot describe it." This comes even from people who have a
large vocabulary. Heretofore man expressed his noblest self in
dance and gesture, until the word-mongers put him to sleep
with their dreary drugs and grabbed the ordering and gover-
nance of ritual for themselves. Then "The Word" was made
more important than the act, so that now religion is a doleful
mumbling in church pews and the philosophy of life is a tan-
gle of incomprehensible phrases in a book.

The dancer and artist deplores this tendency to restrict the expression of the grandest impulses of humanity to agitations in the larynx and to words and more words in a book. The dancer believes that his art has something to say which cannot be expressed in words or in any other way than by dancing. He recognizes that he is the lineal descendant of those ancients who expressed their innermost feelings in dance and gesture long before language became common.

He is, in a sense, a throwback. He is aware of that but believes that his art is rooted so deeply in Man's fundamental instincts that he can read back into His unconscious re-membrance, before the atrophy of civilization set in, and move Him profoundly without a word being spoken. This is so little recognized among laymen that such a conversation as this, between a college girl and myself, took place recently:

She asked—"How much do professional dancers have to study?" On my replying that students often dance five or six hours a day for several years, she said: "I don't mean the steps, but really study, you know, from a book." To me this is both horrifying and pathetic. There are times when the simple dignity of movement can fulfill the function of a volume of words. There are movements which impinge upon the nerves with a strength that is incomparable, for movement has power to stir the senses and emotions, unique in itself. This is the dancer's justification for being, and his reason for searching further for deeper aspects of his art.

But the reaction of his potential audience, except for a few, puts the artist in the position of having to defend and explain. Actually very few people understand the basic element of the dancer's art, or appreciate the impulse which provokes the modern dancer to enlarge it. Yet the explanation is quite simple if the reader will try to forget his prejudices, and examine his reactions to movement of any kind, and then translate it into terms of dancing.

MOVEMENT SPEAKS VOLUMES: KINESTHESIA IS THE WORD FOR IT

Who, for instance, has not felt a thrill of violence as a train rushes past, or not experienced the quieting effect of still

water? These sensations are examples of the two extremes of
our response to movement; on the one hand, the terror inspired
by movement out of our control; on the other hand, the negative response we have to absolute rest. Neither sensation in its
ultimate sense is emotionally bearable, the one being confusing, the other boring. Between the two, however, lies a whole
range of movement with definite degrees of stimulation and
response. Allied to this response to the static and the dynamic
is the response to balance and unbalance. John Martin, in his
"American Dances," has explained this phase of my work in
the following words:

> In its structural sense, movement is "The arc between two
> deaths." On the one hand is the death of negation,
> motionless; on the other hand is the death of destruction,
> the yielding to unbalance. All movement can be consid-
> ered to be a series of falls and recoveries; that is, a delib-
> erate unbalance in order to progress, and a restoration of
> equilibrium for self-protection. Thus is typified the basic
> life struggle for maintenance and increase. A more dra-
> matic medium, or more inseparable from human experi-
> ence could hardly be imagined; it is inherently both excit-
> ing and relevant. The nearer the state of unbalance
> approaches the dangerous the more exciting it becomes
> to watch, and the more pleasurable the recovery. This dan-
> ger zone, which life tends to avoid as much as possible, is
> the zone in which the dance largely has its existence.

The only author on esthetics I have ever read who perceived
this same fundamental relationship of balance and unbalance to
all art, is Ozenfant, the French painter and teacher who, in a
chapter on "Constants," in his book *Foundation of Modern Art,*
shows a diagram of a man falling and states that all form is the
echo in us of the awareness of gravity, and that the unconscious
participation in the constant falling and recovering of all moving objects is the basis of a universal language of feeling. Not a
word about dancing as the supreme manifestation of this language occurs in the book. In fact, no mention is made of the
dance whatever. In this respect, M. Ozenfant is in complete

accord with at least ninety-nine percent of the world's authors
of books on art. This obtuseness on the part of authors is a
tempting subject, but being far too busy to pursue, single-
handed, a fight with esthetes who ignore the dance as the
mother of the Arts, I had best proceed with an explanation of
the stuff the Dance is made of.

The sense which perceives and responds to the stimuli of
balance and unbalance, stasis and movement, is rooted in the
muscles and is known to dancers and students of physiology as
Kinesthesia. It is the Modern Dancer who claims by instinct
and training, to have a special consciousness of kinesthesia. For
him it is an instrument for promoting an esthetic experience
appealing to senses to which no other art appeals. Not only
this, but the special claim of the Modern Dancer is that he, and
only he, by painstaking search, has rediscovered and re-applied
the laws of kinesthesia so that the dancer appears as a human
being on the stage and not a machine for making geometrical
lines in space. Or, rather, this is what I claim that I do.
Unfortunately, it is not possible to assert that all modern dancing looks human and not geometric. In general, however, it
would be easier for a theological student to deny God than for
the dancer to deny the existence of kinesthesia. His special perception of it makes it imperative for him to use it. That is why
he dances instead of writing a book.

Kinesthesia is a rudimentary response in most people, and
there is a great need for a fuller consciousness of this special
sense for it to be ordered and made comprehensive. Only thus
can audiences really enjoy modern dancing. This sense needs to
be enlarged by education and training; nothing else about us
has been so much allowed to atrophy. When man ceased to run
and leap for his food the decay of the kinesthetic sense began.
With this defection the universal interest in dance and ritual
also declined, and as man labored slowly outwards and upwards
to the heaven of industrial civilization where his food comes
with the nuts and bolts of the assembly line, so did he lose any
sympathetic perception of dance movement which extends
beyond the piston one-two of the Rockettes' leg drill.

But this situation is not entirely hopeless. The further increase in leisure time arising out of our industrial growth has helped to increase play and athletics and most particularly the ballroom dance and the folk dance. These will partially restore to the layman some of the perceptiveness of his kinesthetic sense.

DANCING IS LIKE MUSIC

One of the things that makes the language of kinesthesia difficult from the dark side of the footlights is that it is abstract. Its scope is roughly parallel with that of music. Like music, it has psychic overtones to which one responds and which give one definite emotions not clearly described. This in the dance is called Metakinesis, or emotional meaning overlaying kinesthesia, and can be the whole reason for a dance; for a dance composed without any story does have, for whoever looks for it, a great deal of meaning. This meaning is for him alone; that is, it belongs with those profound, almost incomprehensible, responses within us, of which we can scarcely tell because they defy the telling.

Everyone is familiar with these strong but difficult-to-define responses when it comes to music. The symphony, for example, is abstract; it does not tell a story, yet great masses of people are profoundly stirred by the marvellous interplay of tone, rhythm, melody and harmony. These elements in the hands of a great composer recall experience, purge and elevate the spirit, and, by organizing harmony against disharmony, help to make the tragedy of living bearable. The very fact that music such as this is abstract makes it powerful. Each one who listens may interpret the sounds in his own way; it speaks to him directly, unhampered by a certain kind of circumstance. The traditional contrast to this is Opera, where the intricacies of the plot may interest you; on the other hand, they may distract you from the music and your personal drama. Then again, the appearance of a real pair of lovers—in *Tristan and Isolde*—may meet your demands of romantic love but often it is more thrilling to listen to the music either canned or on the concert stage.

Abstract dancing is analogous to abstract music. The same elements are there—the tone, rhythm, melody and harmony,

with the addition of the kinesthetic appeal only possible in the
dance. This means that, to a sensitive onlooker, there is a constant stream of primitive excitement going on inside him;
movement and gestures by the dancers, that have been sub-
merged in his subconscious mind, seem to come alive in him;
he is young, supple, strong. He sees re-enacted urges and releas-
es that he has had only words for, efforts and successes, and fail-
ures, all more dynamic for being expressed in movement. He
sees models of dynamic equilibrium; units running, falling,
leaping, whirling, not disintegrating but always balancing out
into a logical continuity of creative line. Or perhaps the choreographer will give him, as a contrast, the horrid bogeyman—
Disharmony—staggering drunkenly through a group where
freedom means anarchy, and the conflicting elements do not
yield to logic and reason. Again, the mass pattern of the dance
may hold the mirror up to humanity. It can indicate its vulgar
grimacing images, scrambling and competing in wild riotous
disorder. It catches the audience in the theatre in a sober and
reflective mood and shows it the image of the drunken, orgiastic confusion which is optimistically called Civilization, and to
which it returns once it steps outside. It is like playing to an
alcoholic a victrola record of his previous night's indiscretions.
Before the audience leaves, however, the dancer gives it an
object lesson in the smoothness of line, beauty of form, and
clarity of purpose a group can achieve by the co-ordination of
its parts and the mutual co-operation of the individuals composing the group. Again, for instance, the aspect of the eternal
triangle is presented in its abstract form. The bickering of the
opposed A, B and C becomes a jarring rhythm creating a feeling of discomfort in the audience and the resolution of the triangle in terms of harmony, because it is pleasurable, creates an
intellectual bias towards such a solution.

WHAT DOES IT MEAN TO YOU?

Sometimes the interpretation by an audience is quite different
from what the choreographer intended, but this does not disturb
him in the least, or, shall I say, it does not disturb me. An A, B,

and C theme may mean international complications to some. This is quite alright as long as it means something to them. I don't even mind the quite far-fetched explanation such as the one that came to my ears about my "Bach Passacaglia in C Minor." At a certain point in this abstract composition one dancer walks on the backs of certain others with an heroic and rather haughty stride. The left wing said this was Capitalism walking on the backs of Labor, and when Labor finally arose and dominated the scene, their joy was complete. The idea I had used was Courage and Faith in the face of adversity. Far from being contrite over the charge, which I frequently have from critics, that such and such an abstract dance is vague, and that it might mean different things to different people, I say let them fit the dance into their own experience; this is the power and the glory of abstraction. Must Cesar Franck's symphony be about Adolphe, who was sitting one day in a garden overlooking the Rhine, when Anna, a beautiful young girl, walks by, reminding him of his lost love in the Bavarian Alps? Only if you are ten years old I should think.

I wonder if any of this will answer the lady from Oklahoma?

RANDOM REMARKS

Charles Weidman
1901–1975

*I*n 1921 Charles Weidman found his way to Denishawn from Lincoln, Nebraska, and became a member of the company, performing frequently as Martha Graham's partner. It was at Denishawn also that he met Doris Humphrey, which led to an association that lasted more than twenty years.

As a choreographer he is best known for his satirical and whimsical comedies. However, he also created important dances on serious subjects and choreographed several Broadway shows. Like Miss Humphrey, he had an infallible sense of good theater. He also had a natural spontaneity of expression and the ability to single out human traits.

Following the breakup of the Humphrey-Weidman Company, his artistic and personal life began to decline, although he continued to maintain a school and choreograph for his own company and for the New York City Center Opera. After reaching a devastatingly low point in the mid-1950s, he sought to rebuild his career. He opened a new studio, the Expression of Two Arts, which was a miniature replica of the old Humphrey-Weidman Studio Theatre. There, in an inadequate space, surrounded by a few loyal followers, he kept alive his old works and choreographed new ones. The last years before his death brought a new wave of support from the dance world.

Charles Weidman, more a doer than a writer, made the following statement for the second edition of The Dance Has Many Faces (1966).

I have always believed that the audience and the performer are indivisible. Both artist and audience enter the house—although

through different doors—from the same street. They have both seen the same headlines, left the same world of reality behind them. And while the artist puts on his make-up, the audience leaves its everyday disillusionment in the checkroom.

Real art can never be escape from life. In histrionic terms, illusions are not false impressions or misconceptions of reality. The world of illusion which the audience expects from the artist is, in fact, the world of their real selves, the image of their own world, the translation of their hopes and fears, their joys and sufferings into the magic of the stage.

The artist must not run away from himself, from his "center of being." He is the bearer of a message, and it is his responsibility to tell it—in whatever medium it may be—intelligibly, forcefully and with his utmost artistic ability. He may sometimes fail in the delivery of his message, but he must never fail in his purpose.

It is often said of the modern dance that it is not easily understood, that its silent language of movement is so intricate as to veil its meaning. But since any dance presentation lives only while it is being performed and since it can hardly be preserved for later in files and books, it would utterly fail to accomplish its task or even to justify its existence could it not clearly convey its message. Only poets, musicians, painters or sculptors can dare challenge their contemporaries with their media of art and yield to the judgment of posterity. The dancer can do this as little as can the actor or singer. L'art pour l'art is for him the death sentence expressed by his own feeble attempt to convince his audience.

I have always been impatient with the "art pour l'artist." Clarity and understandability has remained the basis of my dance creations. Their intent, concerned with human values and the experience of our times, must be carried by the fullest emotional impact the artist can muster. Then, with the conception of the idea, the intelligibility of its message and the emotional intensity of presentation, the artist's primordial task is fulfilled and—however his artistic deliverance may be judged—his sincerity cannot be doubted.

Some may say that I am going too far when I desire to make

my dance creations as easily understandable as a movie. But this may explain why more and more I have come to believe in the pantomimic dance drama. The word "pantomime" does not mean to me the presentation of a dumb show, as most dictionaries define it, or the mere telling of a story or action without the use of explanatory words. To me it is the transport of an idea into movement, the animation of the feeling behind the idea, an animation in which suddenly all commas and periods, all silent moments of an unwritten play become a reality in movement. Moreover, it may be likened to that emotional sequence of a growing world of images which we may experience when listening to a symphony, full of logical continuity and expressiveness where words might seem feeble and music inadequate.

I may be prejudiced in favor of the pantomimic dance, because I have found that my gift as a dancer is essentially tied up with my dramatic talent as an actor, or—let us better say—as a mime. The modern mime must be a modern dancer, and as such his entire body must be alive. This cannot be acquired by emotional experience, only by hard physical training. It may be best called bodily awareness. In order to test this bodily awareness in one of my dance compositions, I went so far as to exclude the face, i.e., the facial expression, completely from the pantomimic presentation.

Any idea being projected produces its specific movement and gesture pattern which is, in itself, purely abstract. Though, basically, pantomime is not mere storytelling, a story may be, and usually is, achieved by what is done. But to attain such ends, the means must be determined by strict form, since form alone leads to artistry.

In seeking to reach my audience and to convey my message in the easiest understandable manner, I often chose the channels of humor. There are various kinds of humor, but first and foremost it must be said that, whenever a humorous element is required, it can come only from the performer himself and must be projected by him.

In the beginning I employed the most obvious humor, the sadistic type of humor, the effect of which is almost guaranteed with every audience. However, with time, I was continually looking for a broader expression of what I wanted to achieve, and I attempted to abstract the essence of any emotion projected through movement. Here is an example. Instead of being frantic as, let us say, a minstrel would be when a bucket of water is thrown over him, I tried to convey the same idea without impersonating a minstrel and with no bucket of water causing the emotion. This attempt finally crystallized into a dance called *Kinetic Pantomime*. In this composition I so juggled, reversed and distorted cause and effect, impulse and reaction that a kaleidoscopic effect was created without once resorting to any literary representation.

It has been a long and arduous way from this comedy pantomime to Thurber's *Fables*. But my basic approach to subject matter, though it has widened and developed, has never changed. Content and form are equally important to my choreographic pantomimes. I have never believed that artistry can be achieved without adhering to the strictest form, nor that the heart of the public can be reached, if the artist is blind to the life that surrounds him or tries to shut himself off from it by escaping into mere fantasy and romance. Art demands that we be part of life and merge with it. Art and life are as indivisible an entity as the artist and his audience.

HANYA SPEAKS

Hanya Holm
1893–1992

*T*he German dancer, Hanya Holm, along with Martha Graham, Doris Humphrey, and Charles Weidman participated in the Bennington College School of the Dance in the 1930s. She was actually a second-generation modern dancer, having been a member of the Wigman company in Germany. The success of Mary Wigman's first tour in the United States in 1930 and 1931 encouraged her to ask Holm to come to America in 1931 to establish a New York branch of the Wigman school. Holm developed her own school, company, and style, successfully adopting German modern dance principles to American dynamics and temperament.

Although forced to disband her company in 1944, Holm continued to maintain a studio in New York. Choreographically, she turned to musical comedy on Broadway, her best-known contribution being My Fair Lady. Her former students, who include Alwin Nikolais, Don Redlich, Nancy Hauser, and Valerie Bettis, retained in their own work much of that which is unique in German modern dance, particularly the space concepts.

Holm taught at Juilliard, the Nikolais-Louis studio, and Colorado College well past the age of 90. Exploring until the end of her life, she maintained, "You will find out that one life is not enough. You will want to have several lives in which to discover what there is to be discovered."

"Hanya Speaks" deals largely with Hanya Holm's philosophy as a teacher of dance.

You are your own master and student. There is no value in copying what someone else has done. You must search within your own body. What you discover there will be for your own benefit. Others can give you the means, the tools, but they cannot do it for you. The art of dancing is in no book, nor can you take it with a spoon or in [the] form of pills. Dance can only result from your own concentration and understanding. When you do stretches, sit-up exercises, or whatever you may be doing, you are doing it for one one purpose only: you want to make an instrument out of what is otherwise a mere body.

* * *

There is a difference between acting a movement and actually doing it. In the final analysis it is meaningless to count the amount of jumps you can do, because one small gesture which is right and proves the oneness of purpose in what is being done will far outweigh everything else.

* * *

Finding something is the greatest thing that can happen to you. If you are searching you will make new discoveries, but searching is not easy. You cannot help facing movement blocks that will stand in your way. No one can remove these blocks except you yourself, and only when you are able to remove them will you eventually discover yourself. This is the only way you can improve and grow into something big.

* * *

You need an enormous amount of inspiration within yourself. Don't wait for someone to light a candle within you or place a bomb under you. A bomb causes external excitement which is quite the opposite from the excitement you should have. The excitement must come from your inner focus. There can be no inner focus if you are not aware of what the head is doing, what the arm, the trunk, the back is doing. The entire body must be knowledgeable before there can be an inner focus. The same moment you discover that focus you will burst forth in your outward appearance. Your audience will recognize it immediately. The people won't have to look inside of you for emotional overtones. Your chest will be right, your hip will be right, you will have a carriage that is supported and that is right for that which is intended.

* * *

Let's face it, the art of dance is much bigger than any one of us. We are ants in relation to what dance is, but it is an honor to be that ant. Don't say, "Oh well, we did that, and I kicked my leg five inches higher than she did." Who cares? Did you understand the movement? That is what matters.

* * *

Don't swallow everything hook, line, and sinker. Absorb! React! There isn't such a thing as "the" gospel. Don't expect a compliment unless you deserve it. When you do receive a compliment take it at its face value. Good dance instructors do not throw around compliments. They don't throw them away. If you are dissatisfied because of lack of praise, see why you are dissatisfied. Is it the teacher's fault or yours?

* * *

Your enemies are not those about you in the studio, but your own imperfections. You can't fight yourself if you run away and refuse to see yourself.

* * *

On stage there is no use pretending you are an ostrich with your head in the sand. The audience recognizes everything you are trying to hide. Every gesture you make reveals something of you. Don't think you can hide behind a gimmick, or a little bit of extravaganza you have learned to master with great flourish. Even the simplest movement will be marvelous if it is fulfilled by you, by your real self. When you dance you are naked.

* * *

There is no easy short cut to learning how to dance. Don't walk around lamenting that you "didn't feel right, or you didn't feel this or that, or the movement wasn't right for you, or you were out late last night." You have no excuse. You must function right there where the demand is made. Your whole life with its ups and downs must be focused. This doesn't mean that you have to live like a bird in a cage. On the contrary, open up and fly out. That little magnet in the center holds you together. Master whatever comes your way and enjoy the mastering. Unless you are challenged there is no work, there is no accomplishment, there is nothing of value, there is no test of your strength. Strength has to be challenged, otherwise it is lost. Challenges are just as important to life as eating, perhaps even more so.

* * *

Watch little children when they hear some music. They throw themselves around and onto the floor and jump up again. They don't get hurt. They don't care. They enjoy it. They fall down a second time and roll over and laugh it off. You should be able to do the same thing but you kill it with fear. They have no fear. Art is living. It is not just craftsmanship, it is the flow of love. There is that meeting place of the body and the soul and the spirit that gives you control.

* * *

A walk is of no value unless it is of the nature that you can change it. You should be able to do an angry walk, a floating walk, a sombre walk, a determined walk cutting into space. You must be able to change it to fulfill the inner demand of what you want the walk to be. If you can follow only one pattern which is very thoroughly ingrained in you, then you have closed the doors to all of that which is expressional.

* * *

What you are capable of is so marvelous that it is almost impossible to imagine what you could do if you achieved it. Don't say you can never get there. Get as far as you can with a full heart and with full conviction, then try to drive on a little further. To achieve something takes strength. You are not born with that strength, you have to gain it. Don't look at your exercises as something to make your muscles hurt, but as something that will help you to improve yourself. Know that you are a human being, that you are able to take life as it is. Life is not an escape. It is not an excuse. It is not idle cowardliness. You must think, "I can do more this year than I did last year because I have grown meanwhile." Don't dull yourself with copying something or someone, remember that sometimes you absorb much more through your pores than through your head.

* * *

You must be humble in relation to your steady progress. Be thankful for what you have but recognize that you haven't gotten it all. We are all but a small part of what remains to be discovered, to be found out. Those who have attained even a great deal know that there still lie out there somewhere a thousand things yet to be discovered. You will find out that one life is not enough. You will want to have several lives in which to discover what there is to be discovered.

* * *

The right way of developing is to go at a steady pace and to get the most out of every situation. When you have reached a platform, look for the stairs leading up to the next platform. But be patient, don't want success too fast. Learn to wait. The platform on which you stand must not be an illusion. Above all, it must be deserved. It is impossible to remain for very long on a high platform if you don't have an absolute knowledge of what you are doing. Operate within your own ability. Do not try to conquer things which are too far above you. They may kill you. Sooner or later it will show that you have no base, that you are just a hollow front. Audiences are very cruel with hollow fronts. They will say, "Show me!" and if you don't show them they will let you fall flat two miles down to your death. Go the straight, direct way, don't skip anything. Never think that you are better than anyone else. It is the nature of our existence on this earth that no one is better than anyone else.

* * *

At the end of the forties when George Balanchine moved with his company into the City Center, we had long meetings together, and I favored the idea of making a corps of ballet dancers and a corps of modern dancers. There were many talented people in and around New York City, and I wanted to bring them together to form a company for which various choreographers of the modern dance would come in and choreograph with the pool of chosen dancers. The ballet accomplished this but the modern dance did not. The various choreographers would not let go of the members of their companies. This kind of isolationism among modern dance choreographers has caused the audiences to take sides, and thereby modern dance has failed to achieve recognition as a unit. It was planned to include all styles of choreography in the company—so this was not their reason for holding back. The problem was that their ego[s] would not allow them to let go of the group of dancers they had clustered around themselves. About fifteen years later the same attempt was made, the same people came together and wanted to pool a group of dancers, but they could not get the necessary financial backing. No one was willing to take the risk. Modern dance had done too thorough a job of scattering itself in a thousand different directions.

* * *

You can do a lot with very little if you only know how. If you have something of value, if you have a plan, if you know what you are undertaking, if you have the intelligence to do it, you can accomplish it with very little help. If you can prove that you have something, the help will come.

* * *

If you haven't the knowledge to implement a modern dance program, teach folk dance. Folk dance has form, organization, step patterns, relationships, and continuity. It is wrong to try to abstract when you don't even know what the word means. I constantly see abstractions of themes that are nothing more than miserably performed, dull conceptions of what the theme means. Do the forms that can be done at your level. An Irish jig takes great skill. A Yugoslavian folk dance is very difficult to accomplish. These are good forms which you can do if you lack the knowledge of making up your own. One should not look down on the forms established in folk dancing. Folk dancing is a highly developed skill. Skilled folk dancers have the feeling for rhythm and understand the responsibility one has to a beat and a pulse. You should see them do sword dances, you should watch the position of their feet. They are beautiful. If you can accomplish all of this, you are well on your way to becoming a good modern dancer.

* * *

I will never forget the great experience I had in the Cathedral in Strasbourg. It was dark inside the Cathedral so that you could not see clear to the top. It had the effect of funneling your whole attention upward. Light was coming through a beautifully painted window and caused a stream of reflection which hit an altar with a crucifixion scene. It had the most unbelievable effect of arresting your step, of making you stand still, of giving you a heightened sense of being. How many times does this happen? I have been in St. Peter's in Rome and in all of the major cathedrals in Europe but none struck me with that kind of meaningful space. There was a tension inside that church which created the constant feeling of being uplifted.

* * *

Your dances must be built from something within your self. It does not have to be concrete. It may be a very intangible thing. It may have a very wonderful, ethereal reason. You cannot do a dance and then decide what it is. Form has to come out of that to which it is related. That which causes the behavior determines the form.

* * *

If a decoration is placed on a basic structure without feeling for the structure, it will be destructive. Decoration should be used only if it serves to enhance the form and brings out more than the basic naked form can do by itself. Some forms need a diversified statement. Others do not because they are self-sufficient. You must train your senses, taste, and judgment. Training means experience. Judgment is not learning what is black and white.

* * *

Life cannot be superimposed upon a piece of art. If it doesn't have it, it will never have it. The message of life must be given a work at birth. It is the same with us. If we do not have it, we will never have it. We cannot learn it out of a book, it must be learned by experience. It comes with the fine things like the fragrance of a rose.

* * *

Art is projected through the clarity of its form. It is the sum total of something. Something spiritual comes across which is not broadcast through the deed itself, but is manifested in the manner in which you did it. The "how" in which you do it is extremely important. It requires discipline.

* * *

Form is the shape of a content. Form without content becomes form for the sake of form. Inspiration has to be there to make a form live. The form should contain the original impetus out of which it was created. If the form emerged from an emotional ingredient, then that emotional ingredient must be there.

* * *

You should not dance academically. It has no departure, no breath, no life. The academician moves within a group of rules. Two plus two are four. The artist learns rules so that he can break them. Two plus two are five. Both are right from a different point of view.

* * *

An example: a rule is that your knee has to be over your toe when you perform a plié. Sometimes you have to turn the knee in and break the rule. If you know the rule and technique, then you can bring that knee in without getting hurt. For some things the knee must be in in order for the shape and form to be right according to that which you are communicating. Another rule is that when walking you transfer the weight from straight knee to straight knee with an adjustment of the general velocity. You may want to walk in an awkward way with hanging knees for the reason of getting an idea across. You have broken the rule of walking right, but you have entered a form through which you could communicate. Yet if you don't know the rules you won't know how to break them. You might make the baggy knees the norm and the shuffling forward the rule. If you don't know the rules you won't know what to go away from, and there are millions of departures. Your form will often demand that you break rules.

* * *

There are a thousand points of view. Hindemith and I were at the same conservatory in Frankfurt. We both received the same kind of basic training. Then he departed in the way of finding out how music could be made. He used combinations of many different kinds, the twelve-tone scale, the cacophony, the dissonances, broad chords requiring more than ten fingers. He became absorbed in tone qualities and the tone relationships of intervals, but before he died he came back to the classic style. You can work, for example with just the hands and arms and develop them to the *n*th degree until they are marvelous—but you will come to a dead end where it will be necessary to return to the body in order to incorporate your findings into the body as such in order to go on moving.

* * *

There are books written about circles and squares. The ancient people understood them. You will find them amongst the old Egyptian ruins. Some of the old Mayan ruins were temples with a circle or a square of stone tops which were of great significance. No one originated these forms. They have always existed. One day while walking about Rome I came upon a church called St. Clement. There was an entrance at one of its

sides leading downstairs. Two flights below the church was an
ancient heathen worship ground. After passing several hallways
which were very low, I came to a chamber with seats around
the outside. In the center was a square altar. The old mystical
signs were still visible everywhere in the room. They had been
hammered into the stone. The worshipers had worn away the
earth where they had been sitting. On top of this chamber was
a very common assembly hall and on top of that was the
church. The more intelligent the ancient peoples were, the
more mystical was the form in its use and significance. There is
more to a round than just making a circle. You will have to run
in circles for many days before you will know what a circle is.
Then all of a sudden you will realize that you are not yourself
anymore, that your space is dynamic and powerful and that you
have to master that force. Turning is almost a dervish exercise
with the world suddenly going around and you feeling very
calm and quiet. If you work for half a year on circles, your turns
will become different.

* * *

Style requires a certain form, and you have to stick to that
form. You have to discipline yourself to it, or you will not get
a good theater piece. The characteristic has to be maintained in
every aspect of the work. Even a walk has to be practiced.
There are a thousand walks. If you don't know which walk to
do, you will just wobble and walk as best you can, but nothing
will be created by it. A walk without a characteristic is as good
as nonexistent, it is pitiful. It would be better to lower the curtain and go home.

* * *

The line between emoting and emotion is different with
each person. You have to discover within yourself when your
technique arrives at a point where your movement becomes an
experience as such. You must master the physical experience so
that it becomes a kinesthetic experience. You will discover
through this kinesthetic experience that a relationship is established within the body which coordinates the flow of move-

ment and the flow of animation. You will find out that movement can contain only a certain amount of emotion before the
emotion outdoes the physical experience. When this overtaxa-
tion happens, you have overdrawn. Emotion is a stimulus, not
an end result. It is arrived at but not emphasized. Emotion is
the stimulus which gives the movement its coloring, its reason
for being. Since the emotion is the stimulus for the movement,
it is, therefore, both the stimulus and a part of the end result.

* * *

The face is of course the mirror of all that goes on, but it
should not be more prominent than is intended and it should
not substitute for all that which isn't going on in the body.
Facial muscles are very small and very sensitive. If the face does
too much it turns into mugging. The face becomes a thing in
itself. It overdoes things because the body doesn't understand
what to do and therefore the face substitutes. The face should
have a relationship to the whole attitude. It should enliven the
attitude and complement it. A dancer's face is not a mask. I
sometimes look at the eyes instead of looking at the movement
and I very often see absolutely dead eyes inside a multiple-
moving body.

* * *

Your body is your language. Cultivate your language. Be able
to say what you want. If you are supposed to be in second position with your bottom sticking out, then it is right according
to the form. If your bottom is not supposed to be sticking out
and it is, it is an insult to the form. The form is changed from
a form into nothing. A form is a silent thing which has
achieved a shape. The shape will be as exciting as that which
you put into it. It will be clear only as you give it clarity. It can
have only the shape which you give it. It can achieve life only
because you have given it such. The responsibility is yours.

* * *

Check yourself and see if you are willing to sacrifice yourself for something that is bigger than you are. You must know

to what you have put your mind. If you are in dance just to sat-isfy your ego, then be a nice admirer but get out of the field. If you are dabbling in dance just for your own satisfaction, go right ahead, but don't pass on your half-knowledges to people who are searching. Dance is the noblest art there is. Sacrifice is necessary, even if that sacrifice is your ego. This does not mean that you should become a limp rag and let everyone wipe his dirty feet on you. Your inner self must give you hope, strength, belief, a power of dedication without resorting to the ugly thing of cheating. Make-believes are not worth anything; they have their own doom written within themselves; they only wait for you to find out, and by the time you do find out you will have wasted years and years and years. Waste you must, but waste in the right direction.

* * *

The inner man is a fine little point where your being comes together. If you could externalize it, it would not be bigger than the head of a pin. In size of volume it is not a fraction of a fraction of an atom. This inner man is like the center of a hur-ricane. The secret of a hurricane is its eye. The eye is calm. If you destroy that eye you destroy the hurricane. If you can't be as calm as the eye of the hurricane which holds all the answers to the devastating storm of the outside, you can't hold yourself up in the world of dilemma and battle. There is no force that does not come from an utter calm. Sensitivity, the power to absorb and to register, is the calm of the eye which starts that outer passion and tremor.

* * *

When you have discovered that inner self, you can call your-self a dancer, but don't get snooty about it. Dancers don't live in ivory towers. If you put that inner man on a scale, it wouldn't weigh more than a hundredth of an ounce. The more you know, the humbler you become, if you really know it. This is growing, studying, living. Dance is life. Know that you are alive.

Part Three

THE SECOND
GENERATION

INTRODUCTION

The first of the second-generation performing groups was a unit of the Workers Dance League, which had been started in the early thirties by students of the New York Wigman School. Concerned for the social ills of the world, they gave performances in trade union halls for labor groups and gained the support of the Communist Party. Over the next ten years many young dancers joined the group, during which time it lost its radical leanings. It had become the New Dance Group, from which evolved in 1942 the performing trio of Jane Dudley and Sophie Maslow of the Martha Graham Company, and William Bales of the Humphrey-Weidman Company. Their New Dance Group Studio offered modern dance classes in a variety of styles, and continues into the present as an eclectic training ground.

Many of the early members of the second generation began choreographing independently while they were still members of the parent dance company. Among them were José Limón and Sybil Shearer of the Humphrey-Weidman Company, Valerie Bettis of the Hanya Holm Company, and Anna Sokolow, Merce Cunningham, and Erick Hawkins of the Martha Graham Company. Interestingly, in spite of a continuing philosophical rejection of ballet, some of these dancers studied it and used certain aspects of it in their own techniques.

Opportunities for younger dancers began to grow. In 1936 the first series of Sunday afternoon concerts at the 92nd Street Young Men's Hebrew Association in New York City was instituted, offering young dancers a setting in which to make their debuts. Classes were also held at the YMHA, enhancing its position as a center for modern dance. In 1940 the Humphrey-Weidman Company opened a studio theater in which to give their performances, and also made it available to younger dancers.

In 1948 the Bennington School of the Dance was reinstituted at Connecticut College, with Martha Hill and Ruth Bloomer as codirectors. With better performing and studio facilities than those that had been available at Bennington, modern dance had a new summer home.

During the fifties, efforts were directed toward bringing modern dance to larger audiences. The Martha Graham Company had already performed in Broadway theaters, and other companies began to follow suit. Indeed, they were virtually forced to do so in order to be reviewed in the two influential newspapers, *The New York Times* and the *New York Herald-Tribune*. Touring to colleges and universities surpassed prewar levels as the strength and budgets of college dance programs grew.

Most dance companies continued to operate on a shoestring although, for some, increased recognition brought welcome financial assistance. For the first time, foundations began giving grants to a few modern dancers, although most of the money still went to ballet companies. Beginning in 1954, some modern dance companies found themselves used as instruments of U.S. foreign policy by giving State Department–sponsored tours. In fact, for the next fifteen years the Martha Graham Company was not seen in the United States outside of New York City. On the whole, it seemed that the financial problems of modern dance companies were lessening and that the art form had indeed arrived.

During the decade of the 1950s, men began to take over the major leadership of modern dance, despite the continuing social stigma against male participation. José Limón began the José Limón Dance Company in 1947. With Doris Humphrey continuing as his artistic advisor and choreographer until her death, he became one of the most prominent figures in modern dance. He developed a strong, visually striking style for his dances, which were often based on religious or historical themes. As the size of his company grew, he became a master of large group choreography.

In the same period, the avant-garde leaders of modern dance, Merce Cunningham, Erick Hawkins, and Alwin Nikolais, advanced styles that differed widely from one another and from all other dancers. Each had broken away from the style of his mentor (Cunningham and Hawkins had worked with Martha Graham and Nikolais had worked with Hanya Holm). Influenced by other artists, each developed a unique approach to the use of music, sets, costumes, and above all to choreography and movement. Costuming was revolutionized by the invention of Helanca; leotards and tights became the sole costumes, creating the unisex look. In the sixties the Moog synthesizer, the computer, and other electronic devices were used to create new music. Projections of slides onto the stage added a new visual dimension. Sets utilized contemporary materials, such as the helium-filled pillows created by Jasper Johns for Cunningham's *Rainforest.*

Even though these artists became established in the dance world, continued exploration and discovery kept them in the avant-garde of modern dance. Other men also have made significant contributions. Murray Louis, then principal dancer with Alwin Nikolais, continued to perform with the Nikolais company after establishing his own company. A dancer's dancer, often humorous, Louis has a gift for kinetic timing.

Paul Taylor, a former member of the Martha Graham Company, began by experimenting with nondance, in the spirit of the avant-garde. As time passed, however, he explored many diverse styles, some balletic, some highly energetic, others in a narrative vein. His company has become one of the most popular in America.

Alvin Ailey took over direction of the Lester Horton Company for a while after Horton's death in 1953, and then struck out on his own. In blending his African-American heritage with his dance background, he created enormously popular and exciting works, and his choreographic career soared. He went on to establish the Alvin Ailey American Dance Theater, a repertory company, which remains immensely popular after his death.

Of the women of the second generation, Anna Sokolow spent a number of years in Mexico; Sybil Shearer moved to Illinois; Valerie Bettis worked both on and off Broadway; Jean Erdman, Pearl Lang, Mary Anthony, and others had small companies that did not have the impact of the larger ones. Bella Lewitzky of the Horton Company remained in California and created a company of her own.

During this period, modern dance began to evolve from an expression of the human condition to the presentation of movement for its own sake. Many of those who continued in the earlier tradition used dance as an expression of the concerns of mid-twentieth-century America.

YOU HAVE TO
LOVE DANCING TO
STICK TO IT

Merce Cunningham
1919–

*M*erce Cunningham is a maverick. By constant exploration, he has had a far-reaching impact on modern dance. The dances that he has choreographed exist for themselves rather than for expressive content. He has eliminated dependence on music by allowing the dance to coexist with the sound and developed "chance" choreography which avoids usual or expected movement sequences.

Cunningham's dance beginnings seem conventional: tap dance lessons in his hometown of Centralia, Washington. The relatively early influence of avant-garde composer John Cage, who taught at the Cornish School of Music in Seattle while Merce was a student there, has had a lifelong impact on him. His later associations with artists Robert Rauschenberg and Jasper Johns have also been influential.

In 1939 Cunningham attended the Bennington Summer School of the Dance at Mills College. He then went to New York to study with Martha Graham and at the School of American Ballet. Cunningham joined the Graham Company as a soloist in 1940 and performed with her for the next five years. He began choreographing during that time, and established the Merce Cunningham Dance Company in 1953.

Cunningham has coupled a down-to-earth attitude with a sense of humor and an open point of view. He has been a major influence on the avant-garde while continuing to work at the forefront of modern dance. Cunningham has choreographed dances for spaces outside the *theater (notably for museums and gymnasiums), collaborated on a variety of filmdances and videodances, and has been instrumental in the development of computer programs for dance.*

The choreographic philosophy that is expressed in the following statement continues to pervade Cunningham's work.

you have to love dancing to stick to it.   it gives you
nothing back, no manuscripts to store away, no paintings
to show on walls and maybe hang in museums, no poems to
be printed and sold, nothing but that single fleeting
moment when you feel alive.   it is not for unsteady souls.

> and though it appeals through the eye
> to the mind, the mind instantly rejects
> its meaning unless the meaning is
> betrayed immediately by the action.
> the mind is not convinced by kinetics
> alone, the meaning must be clear, or
> the language familiar and readily
> accessible.

the kinesthetic sense is a separate and fortunate
behavior.   it allows the experience of dancing to
be part of all of us.

> but clarity is the lowest form of
> poetry, and language, like all else
> in our lives, is always changing.
> our emotions are constantly being propelled by some new
> face in the sky, some new rocket to the moon, some new
> sound in the ear, but they are the same emotions.

you do not
separate
the human being
from the
actions he
does, or
the actions
which sur-
round him,
but you can
see what it
is like to
break these
actions up
in differ-
ent ways, to
allow the
passion, and
it is pas-
sion, to ap-
pear for each
person in his
own way.

it is hard for many people to
accept that dancing has nothing
in common with music other than
the element of time and division
of time.   the mind can say how
beautiful as the music hints at,
or strikes out with color.

but the other extreme can be seen
& heard in the music accompanying the movements of the
wild animals in the Disney films.
it robs them of their instinctual
rhythms, and leaves them as car-
icatures.   true, it is a man-made,
arrangement, but what isn't?

the sense of human emotion that a
dance can give is governed by fam-
iliarity with the language, and the
elements that act with the language;
here those would be music, costume,
together with the space in which the dance happens.

joy, love, fear, anger, humor, all can be "made clear" by
images familiar to our eyes.   and all are grand or meager
depending on the eye of the beholder.

what to some is splendid entertainment,
to others merely tedium and fidgets;
what to some seems barren, to others
is the very essence of the heroic.

and the art is not the better nor the worse.

A LITTLE HOUSE TO UNDERSTAND AND PROTECT IT

Erick Hawkins
1909–1994

*E*rick Hawkins, a native of Trinidad, Colorado, majored in Greek studies at Harvard University and studied ballet before he became a modern dancer. Between 1935 and 1939 he danced with the American Ballet and Ballet Caravan. But in 1938 he joined the Martha Graham Company and left his ballet career behind, becoming Graham's principal partner, and later her husband. In 1947 he began to choreograph, and in 1951 he left Martha Graham to establish an independent life and career.

Hawkins developed a theory of dance that is radically different from Graham's, one that emphasizes ease and the free flow of movement, together with an Oriental gentleness. He believed that dance should be a visually sensuous experience. This philosophy pervaded his dances. Contributing to the quality of Hawkins' work has been the influence of his composer and wife Lucia Dlugoszewski and his insistence on using live musicians at his performances.

Hawkins, whose studio and company in New York continue after his death, was one of the most articulate modern dancers. His 1992 book The Body is a Clear Place and Other Statements on Dance reveals the passion and intellect of one of the most respected figures in modern dance. The essay which follows here epitomizes the quality of a Hawkins dance.

Dance today in the western world is an art that has just been born.

Therefore, we have now two pleas: not only for the new image in an established art, but for the new image in a new art.

(Of course, in somewhere and somehow, dance has always existed even in the west, but on the whole stream of ideas of western culture, it has only been a parenthesis.)

Once born, this dance must grow. It cannot be codified and repeated without the delight in its own day to dayness. Its only tradition is to discover truth for that day.

Every day the mystery must be performed.

Yet the mystery is only the same mystery of every day.

The noise outside is deafening. Someone must say, "sshh," "listen!"

No critic can write this vision, that will create young new dancers. No critic can call the modern dance dead. Only the dancer who loves will have the love to see it live, and call out, "Lazarus, come forth!"

Few people are innocent enough to come to a bright light and see the light or anything for we live with eyes shut tight by no's and it often takes the right word to say "open! this is yes!" And what work could anyone propose? Buddha's ultimate word was lifting the flower in his hand. We have had too much honking of horns to understand such silence. Actually only the shouted word is the reigning favorite of our time. Among the Balinese every man dances. Among the Hopis I have seen men from four (when they began) to a clan chief (of ninety-two) dance. Among us what does everyman do? Read the newspaper?

Ever since I was a little boy living in my culture I couldn't help but sense that something was not quite right; that all the answers had not yet been given; that something had not yet been born that desperately needed to be born. It was too much a culture of deadness and deathliness and ugly bodies. I have always wondered whether every child as he or she grows up arrives at a strange and sorrowful disillusionment when he sees the miracle of the body spoiled and degraded in the adult world. Our only image really for the body is equated with pornography. Our image of dance has always been of something we could never be—that of the fat old sultan owning his pretty little dancing girls.

The truth of art has never been the peacock feather to titillate the fat old caesar. It could never be something he could buy, something outside his own body, to really be. And if it were within him, it could never let him be the fat old caesar. Art has *never* been a luxury; always the deepest force to keep us alive. . . (more than any food or drug).

The dance is the truth, within each person's own special body-that-will-never-happen-again (somehow the ourselfness inside the world). This has been the real revolution of modern dance.

Real-ly speaking, the whole nature of the spirit is the creating of beautiful flesh, and to deny the flesh is to *muzzle* the spirit and therefore to deny the spirit.

The "now" of word-poetry and of music has been slightly unhinged by the bookbinder and the recording machine. But dance, more than any other art, still exists only in the "now" and no place else. This might make it less attractive and less profound to our world so bent on hanging on to each hard complacent thing (even though our dying would never understand).

For me, the momentness of dance is one of its most precious gifts. Actually only the nowness of ourselves really exists; that true seeing of time; in the quiver; in the inside of our seeing and not on the outside horribly on the face of a clock. I want to perform that act which we call moving which really is the insides of our seeing. This is what I want to do more than anything else in the world.

But the dance does not occur until the one who watches sees it as well as the one who dances dances it; until the dancer is sitting in the audience as well as standing on the stage.

I am tired of constantly presenting and seeing presented modern dances as some tiny mysterious naked baby without any little house to understand and protect it. I would like to try to build a little house out of the only materials that can really be found lying around in the streets of our culture—the written words. Architects, painters, and composers of the last fifty years have certainly discovered the power of this material to proclaim the birth of their own. Witness: Frank Lloyd Wright and Le Corbusier, Stravinsky and Schoenberg, Kandinsky and Klee. Now is the time for the dancer, the time of now.

Never any more than today has the world needed artists. From the time of Christ, and even before, the oracle has ever told us to be as the little child and enter the kingdom of heaven and yet every day we see some six-year-old dragging his imaginationless sixty-year-old body around before us to destroy us. The little child is disappearing off the face of the earth and only the artist with his deep love can ever hope to resurrect such an image. For even one person to move beautifully would be to give the possibility of beautiful movement to everyone in the world.

For to move beautifully is to be the little child; the human reality at its most total awareness of the material of living more unfixable than the very aliveness of any man's life.

ON DANCE

José Limón
1908–1972

J *osé Limón was born in Culiacan, Mexico, and grew up in Los Angeles. In 1928 he went to New York to study painting, but a performance by the German dancer Harald Kreutzberg so inspired him that he enrolled in classes at the Humphrey-Weidman studio shortly afterward. Limón studied and danced with the Humphrey-Weidman Company from 1930 to 1940. He also began choreographing independently and organized the Little Group, which performed at the Humphrey-Weidman studio. In 1937 he was a recipient of a Bennington School of the Dance Fellowship. From 1940 to 1942 Limón toured the West Coast with May O'Donnell, a former member of the Graham Company. After serving in the U.S. Army during World War II, he formed a trio and placed it under the artistic direction of Doris Humphrey, a position she held until her death. During that time the company grew in size and became one of the major dance companies in the United States.*

Many of Limón's dances reflect his Mexican-American heritage, and some clearly exhibit the love of music that he inherited from his father, who was an orchestra conductor. One of his main concerns was to present "the grandeur of the human spirit and the basic tragedy of man." Limón's dance style was magnificently strong, masculine, and elegant, traits that are apparent also in the following essay.

The Dance is all things to all men. Parents are delighted and amazed at the instinctive response of their infant to music. "Look, he's dancing." Children do not walk to school. They run, skip, hop, leap: they dance to school, or into the dining

room, or up the stairs to bed. The adolescent is notorious for his nervous, jittery dances. And love's young dream: imagine our early romances without a waltz by moonlight! We discover the rapture and intoxication of love during the dance. And even maturity finds a new dimension to the weary business of existence during the sedate ritual of the ballroom: a suspension, a surcease, an inexplicable lifting of the spirit, when even the corns cease to hurt. The dance is an atavism. It has been with us since we became humans, and no doubt even before that. It will be with us to the end. It is a human necessity, profound and not to be denied. Puritans have banned and proscribed it at various times as the work of the Devil, happily without success. I believe that we are never more truly and profoundly human than when we dance.

It is religion. In primitive societies it solemnizes birth, puberty, marriage, and death, the seasons, the sowing and the harvest, war and peace, and to this day in our western world, young boys dance to the Virgin before the high altar in the Cathedral in Seville, and the Indians in Mexico and the Southwest dance their religion.

It is joy. I have seen sober, middle-aged people lose themselves utterly in congas and square dances. Young people would not be young without their dances, those rituals which celebrate the ineffable joy of being alive.

It is pleasure. Think only what musicals would be if you were to leave out the dances, and can you imagine a circus without the dances of the clowns and the acrobats? For certainly the buffoons are dancing. And what the performers on the trapezes and tight ropes do is a very exciting sort of dance.

It is art. Some of the most sublime and creative works of man in the twentieth century have been accomplished by dancers. It is an inspiring panorama, both in Europe, with the traditional dance, and here in this country with the so-called Modern Dance. This latter aspect of the art of the dance, which is the one that I serve, has been referred to by various names, such as the "Serious Dance," the "Concert Dance," the "Creative Dance," etc. It has made some very great contributions to the art. It has influenced greatly the traditional dance.

But I think that its greatest contribution lies in giving the dance to the individual. It has broken with the great orthodoxy of the traditional Ballet, and given validity to personal expression. Since one human being differs from another, this has often led to painful results. But in the case of the disciplined artist, this liberation has given us, in this country, certainly, the most exalted art.

The dancer is fortunate indeed, for he has for his instrument the most eloquent and miraculous of all instruments, the human body. My teacher, Doris Humphrey, when I first came to her studio as an unpromising but dedicated beginner, told us something I have never forgotten. She said, "The human body is the most powerfully expressive medium there is. It is quite possible to hide behind words, or to mask facial expression. It is conceivable that one can dissimulate and deceive with paints, clay, stone, print, sounds. But the body reveals. Movement and gesture are the oldest languages known to man. They are still the most revealing. When you move you stand revealed for what you are."

This great power of expression is ours from the day we are born to the hour of our death. With most human beings it remains largely unconscious. We dancers use this faculty consciously. But it is subjected to long and arduous discipline. The body must be made strong and supple. It is subjected to the exercises of the traditional Ballet and the modern dance techniques to train it in balance, control, elevation, speed, coordination, and exactitude of execution. But to me the most fascinating part of our craft lies in a great search. We explore the possibilities and potentialities for movement inherent in every part of the body. I like to compare it to the symphony orchestra, with its tremendous range and variety of sound, from the robust and percussive to the delicate and subtle. I like to devise exercises and studies which focus on a certain part of the anatomy. This section is isolated, so to speak, and made to move in as many conceivable ways as possible, so that one may become aware of its complete range and capacity, in the same manner that a musical composer must know what each instrument in the orchestra can do. There are exercises, first and foremost, for that great source of movement, the breath center. Then there are others for the shoulders, the ribs, pelvis, knees, feet, elbows, hands, and the head. Each of these regions of the body possesses its own special qualities of movement, and has great possibilities.

Take the head. Leave aside such important means of expression as the eyes and the mouth. The head, from the perpendicular, can be made to hang forward on the chest, or fall backwards as far as the cords of the neck will permit. It can rest sidewise on either shoulder. It can describe a complete circumference, touching the four points just mentioned. Beginning with these simple and rudimentary directions one can devise such complex and endless variations to the movement of the head that, given creativeness and imagination, entire dances can be based on these. The head can be an erect proud symbol, or droop abjectly, or roll in drunken ecstasy and abandonment. It is capable of great pendular convolutions, or infinitely contained, minute gestures. Within its orbit it can move in tilted diagonals, tangents, and obliques, which give it a great expressive range.

The chest can be made empty, to fall inwards and downwards to an utter inversion, a defeat. It can rise with the breath, like a plant growing up and out from the pelvis, and there be suspended, noble and affirmative and aspiring. It can extend beyond this to attitudes of pride and arrogance, and overextend further to the comic, the pompous, the absurd. This region of the chest, the breath, is the fecund source of movement, and its range is limited only by one's inventiveness and imagination.

The shoulder closes forward, and opens backward, and can be lifted or lowered, and made to rotate to describe a full circle. This part of the "orchestra" is capable of small and delicate movement. It can describe with subtlety and nuance.

The area of the ribs can expand and contract, giving the torso great flexibility and fluidity. The ability to bend, to fall away from the balance and poise of the perpendicular into the excitement of the unbalance, the oblique, the wild Dionysian regions, is centered in this part of the body.

The pelvis has a great potency. When it is held in centered

discipline it polarizes the body into a powerful and beautiful column, in perfect harmony with the earth's gravity, serene and Apollonian. From this axis, the pelvis can thrust forward, pull backwards, move from side to side, and describe a complete circumference, and in so doing generate a labyrinth of movement and gesture which can make the body into a graceful object of poetry and lyricism, or break it into crude and violent shapes, discordant and brutal.

In the dramatic language of the dance the use of the knees offers a great paradox. They can project the body into the air, and propel it through space. When locked into a stretched tautness, they raise and suspend the body where it seems to float and deny the pull of gravity. On the other hand, by bending they lower the body to the earth, to a surrender and a death. The inward rotations of the knees create primitive or grotesque attitudes. The outward manipulations lend elegance and expansiveness. The use of the knee-level in the Modern Dance has opened a remarkable new territory. I have seen some stunning passages executed on the knees in the works of Martha Graham and Charles Weidman.

Our contact with the earth with and through the foot gives this part of the dancer a special significance. It is the "radix," and like the roots of plants, it gives the dancer the substance and sustenance of the earth. The use of the foot reveals the entire philosophy of the dance. Surely there is no greater contrast than that between the dance on the points, which seems to etherealize completely the human form, and the use of the bare foot in the contemporary dance. The first came into being through the poetic imagination of the Romantic period, when the dancer was not human, but a supernatural creature borne by the zephyrs. The bare foot came to us through the great rebel, Isadora Duncan. It is a very expressive part of our instrument, supple and beautiful in itself, capable of many more things than being brought to an elegant point. It can be, in the right hands, so to speak, almost as eloquent and expressive as those hands themselves. When emphasis is placed on the heel of the foot a strength and robustness is attained. It can articulate, twist, roll, rotate. It can speak with tenderness or violence.

It has grown to be symbolic of the revolt against the academic dance. Duncan, in her search for a new language for the dance of our time, discarded not only the corsets but the slippers. Her successors in post-World War I Germany and the United States followed in her bare footsteps. In a stricken and turbulent century they created a new language of the dance which could say something about the present world and its tragic realities. The use of the foot in its naked and unfettered beauty was as necessary to the new dance as was the toe-slipper to that of a less disillusioned, less harassed age.

The elbow can articulate in the same fashion as the knee, with the exception that it cannot project the body into the air. It can, however, play an important part in supporting it when the dancer uses the floor level, in falls. This flexible joint gives the arms a rich, flowing quality. The stretching of the joint gives the arm an extended power. The acute bend, with the resultant angularity, opens an entire region of expression, very much related to the cubistic in painting and the dissonant in music. The inward rotations of the flexed or rounded elbow create an inverted, minor tonality in movement, while the opposite, or outward manipulations suggest an open, major one.

One of the most eloquent of the voices of the body is the hand. It is its function to give completion to movement and gesture. The hand is the seal upon the deed. A powerful gesture with the body cannot fully convince unless the hand is in accord with it, nor can a subtle, restrained one be completely so without having the hand in full consonance. The hand can be said to breathe like the lungs. It expands and contracts. It can project movements seemingly to infinity, or gather them back to their source within the body. It is a mouthpiece, a moderator. It has a brilliant range, capable of complexities and subtleties unequaled by other regions of the dancer's "orchestra." It is the abettor of all that the dancer intends. It is unthinkable, a dance without hands.

These are the rich resources of the body. These are the voices. They must be disciplined and developed so that they can speak with truth and power. This necessitates the study of the quality of movement. A single gesture can be phrased in different ways: smoothly, sharply, slowly, rapidly. It can be performed in its entirety, or broken into its component parts. The basic and all-important principle is never forgotten, that movement, in order to have power and eloquence and beauty must spring from the organic center of the body. It must have its source and impulse from the breathing of the lungs and the beating of the heart. It must be intensely and completely human, or it will be gymnastics, and be mechanical and empty. It is this quality, this inflection in the movement that creates that magic in the theater which dance alone can create. Complete mastery of the nuance and color in gesture and movement is the goal toward which the dancer works continually, for this command is what gives his utterance import and validity.

This highly trained, responsible instrument we dedicate to a single idea: that the dance is a serious, adult art, every bit as serious and adult as serious music, painting, literature, and poetry. The oldest of the arts need not exist only as entertainment. It has a great tradition to uphold and by which to be guided and inspired. The American Dance has an imposing gallery of the illustrious. The entire artistic life of the West has felt the impact of Isadora Duncan, the Inceptor. Ruth St. Denis and Ted Shawn pioneered the Wilderness, and took the magic of the dance to the remotest corners of the earth. Their organization was the womb which brought forth Martha Graham, Doris Humphrey, and Charles Weidman. The accomplishments of these children of Denishawn rank with the highest in the cultural story of America. Each has made Art and Civilization in his own very special way. Graham the dark flame, the personifier, the dithyrambic. Humphrey the symphonist, the molder, author of mighty works. Weidman the inspired clown, the Harlequin from the prairie.

These artists have given us something priceless. They have restored the dance to its ancient function, and proven to the modern world that it can reveal, instruct, and ennoble. It can exalt. It can ritualize the great tragedies and ecstasies of man. It is in its power and province to reaffirm the dignity of man in an age that desperately needs this affirmation. Never have the arts been so much needed, nor so challenged, as in these times of mechanized bestiality, when the human species seems possessed by a suicidal frenzy. Surely the Dance can remind us of the greatness of man's spirit, and of his creativeness, not his destructiveness. The Dance is many things. It is a Power. It can help stem the putrefaction and decay gnawing at the heart of human courage, and withstand the philosophies of doom and surrender. The dancer can use his voice to call for reason out of unreason, and order out of disorder. That has always been the high task of the artist. The great Goethe, as death engulfed him, cried "Light, more light." The contemporary artist can do no less than to dedicate the power of his spirit and the flame of his art to bring light to the dark places.

THE REBEL
AND THE
BOURGEOIS

Anna Sokolow
1910–

*T*he daughter of Russian immigrants, Anna Sokolow grew up on the Lower East Side of New York City. Against her mother's wishes, she first studied dance with Bird Larson, then with Blanche Talmud, Martha Graham, and Louis Horst at the Neighborhood Playhouse, at that time located on Grand Street. At the age of fifteen she left home and school to join the Martha Graham Company, with which she performed until 1938.

While a member of the Graham Company Sokolow choreographed and performed independently, beginning in 1933 to present her dances through the Workers Dance League. From the early forties, she spent six months of each year in Mexico, teaching and performing with her company there, the Blue Dove (La Paloma Azul). Sokolow returned to New York in the early fifties and became associated with the New Dance Group, but soon left for Israel to work with the Inbal Yemenite Group. At that time (1953) her performing career stopped. She continues to choreograph for her own repertory company, Anna Sokolow's Players' Project, and on a freelance basis.

Throughout her choreographic career, Sokolow's dances have been based on passionate social comment. Her most famous works include Lyric Suite, Room, Dreams, and Magritte, Magritte.

This essay which was first published in Dance Magazine (July 1966) is a classic statement about modern dance.

I hate academies. I hate fixed ideas of what a thing should be, of how it should be done. I don't like imposing rules, because the person, the artist, must do what he feels is right, what he—as an individual—feels he must do. If we establish an academy, there can be no future for the modern dance. An art should be constantly changing; it cannot have fixed rules.

The trouble with the modern dance now is that it is trying to be respectable. The founders of the modern dance were rebels; their followers are bourgeois. The younger generation is too anxious to please, too eager to be accepted. For art, this is death. To young dancers, I want to say: "Do what you feel you are, not what you think you ought to be. Go ahead and be a bastard. Then you can be an artist."

The modern dance should be non-conformist. We should not try to create a tradition. The ballet has done that, and that's fine—for the ballet. But not for us. Our strength lies in our lack of tradition. Some say that the big change came in the late 1920s, and now is the time for the modern dance to assimilate and solidify. That's all wrong, because it is like building on still another tradition. Without change there can be no growth, and not enough change is going on today.

My quarrel with this generation is that they copy their teachers, and it's their own fault. They don't want freedom; they want to be told what to do. Why don't they realize they don't have to believe everything teacher says? They ought to disagree; they ought to argue.

Of course it's not all the fault of the student. Too often, teachers are merely polite when they should be provocative. They ought to shock. Look at Louis Horst. At eighty, he was still fresh and bold. The good teacher does not teach rules; he stimulates. He shows the students what he knows and inspires them—to go and do something else.

Learning rules cannot produce an artist. What is an artist? What is the nature of the creative process? These are things we can't know; they can't be explained. The creative teacher opens doors for his students to see what life is, what they are. They have to take it from there.

It is easier and quicker to teach by rule, but in the end it's no good. To learn to choreograph, you just have to mess through it for a while. Most people feel they have to "fix" a dance, they have to make it "neat." No—it's better to have disordered life, but to have life. The modern dance is an individual quest for an individual expression of life.

The new generation have not really faced themselves; they don't know what it is they want to say. Most of their choreography is vague. It doesn't come organically from the person. It can't, because the choreographer doesn't know who he is or how he feels. So he tries to cover up his confusion by giving his dances fancy titles, by being intellectual. Dance is not intellectual. It deals with deep emotion.

Choreography always reflects the character of the creator. We see in the person's work what he asks from life and from art. Some want only to be entertained, so they offer us only entertainment. Others see life as a tremendous, mysterious force, and this is reflected in their work. Of course there are times when we want to be entertained. Life is not all deep emotion. Art should recognize all our needs.

I don't believe in ivory towers. The artist should belong to his society, yet without feeling that he has to conform to it. He must feel that there is a place for him in society, a place for what he is. He must see life fully, and then say what he feels about it. Then, although he belongs to his society, he can change it, presenting it with fresh feelings, fresh ideas.

The important thing is that the art being created now be related to now, to our time. The artist must be influenced by his time, conditioned by the life around him. If he is not, his viewpoint is limited by the past, and turns back instead of going forward. If he draws on the ever-changing life around him, his work will always be fresh and new. Art should be a reflection and a comment on contemporary life.

Yet some people are afraid to use life, feeling that art should be something apart, something isolated from reality. I once had a student in Israel who had been in a German concentration camp. You would never have known it from the windblown *schöne tänze* that she composed for me. They amounted to— nothing. I asked her: "Why don't you use your experience?"

Then she created a marvelously powerful study based on the reality she had known.

Anyone, however, can have a good idea for a dance. In itself, that's not enough. There must be form as well as concept; both matter—what you feel—and how you express it. First, the choreographer sees his idea in terms of movement, as the painter sees his in terms of color, line, and mass. This happens spontaneously. Movements are not intellectually contrived but are evoked by emotional images. The only intellectual process is the one that puts these spontaneously conceived movements together into a form that works as whole.

A sense of form, a feeling for construction, can be learned. But there are no rules. How, then? Well, you look at forms, at structures around you. Look at the shape of a box or a bottle; look at the lines of a table. It is easier to see form in life today than it was in the era of the Baroque, when forms were all covered with ornamentation. I don't like elaborated design. I like naked structure. In the theatre, I am anti-décor and anti-costume.

Progress in art comes through the quest for new forms. The artists I most admire are the ones who have dared to break with traditional forms—artists such as Joyce and Picasso and Balanchine. Pure form is not cold, because it is an abstraction from reality; its source is life itself. Form for form's sake is dull, contrived, intellectual. True form comes from reducing reality to its essential shape, as Cezanne did with the apple. In the hands of an artist, form is emotional, exciting. You feel that there is a reason for everything being there, just as it is. There is nothing superfluous, because the artist has stripped his work down to the bare essentials. And an audience responds emotionally to this purity, this inevitability of form, which is beauty.

It takes courage to be so simple. I dig Balanchine because he is daring in his simplicity. Look at the last movement of *Ivesiana*—the dancers just walk on their knees. This is bold; it's modern. It's ballet, but it's modern.

I think there will always be a basic, technical distinction between modern dance and ballet, because the modern conception of training is different. But in dance works there should be no idioms. It's not technique that makes a dance modern;

you can have a modern dance on pointes. It's not subject matter, either. Tudor's *Pillar of Fire* has a romantic story like *Giselle,* but it doesn't reflect the conventional concept of romance. It's a difference in point of view. The modern attitude does not eliminate fantasy or romantic and poetic ideas. But we don't handle them the way the nineteenth century did. We are not representational; we are imaginative.

I have never told stories in dance, though I have always been strongly dramatic. I never plan a dance. I do it, look at it, and then say: "Yes, I see what I am trying to do."

For me, *Lyric Suite* was a turning point. It was then that I began to find a language of movement for myself. I see no reason to fight a personal language; it's an organic statement of the person. But one must not rest on it. The important thing is to stretch the personal vocabulary so that it does not remain static. This does not mean changing its essential nature. One can remain one's self without repeating a statement.

When I first heard the *Lyric Suite,* I was fascinated with Berg's music, because I could see nothing lyric about it. Then it began to evoke dance images for me. After it was done, I saw the first movement as an expression of man; the second, as the quality of woman.

Rooms was choreographed without music. I wanted to do something about people in a big city. The theme of loneliness and noncommunication evolved as I worked. I like to look into windows, to catch glimpses of unfinished lives. Then I ask: "What is there, and why?" Then I thought of using chairs as if they were rooms, each dancer on his own chair, in his own room, isolated from all the others though physically so close to them.

Jazz was the right music for *Rooms.* I have always been interested in jazz; I find it one of the greatest and most profound expressions of our times. It makes me think. In *Rooms,* jazz was used for the dramatic and psychological depiction of individuals. In *Opus 58* I used jazz for an overall aura of the sounds and rhythms of today. I wanted the feeling of a new era, one where life is violent and precarious, and the individual seems unimportant.

Then came *Dreams,* which was my indictment of Nazi Germany. When I started, I had only the idea of dreams, but they became nightmares, and then I saw they were related to the concentration camps. Once this had happened, I intensified the theme by focusing on it.

In *Opus 63* I just started out to do something in unison movement. But the work talked back to me. After a wild Bossa Nova, with everyone going at each other, I ended it with the dancers just walking. It had a quality of strength, like religion; a belief that the spiritual thing will survive. But my works never have real endings; they just stop and fade out, because I don't believe there is any final solution to the problems of today. All I can do is provoke the audience into an awareness of them.

EXCERPTS FROM "NIK: A DOCUMENTARY"

Alwin Nikolais
1910–1993

"***N***ik" was a musician and then a puppeteer before beginning his career in dance, and these roots are reflected in his dances. In them the accoutrements of the theater—lights, props, costumes, sets—are so thoroughly integrated with the movement that the visual result is indeed kinetic art. His dances used mixed media before the term was invented. When modern technology caught up with Nikolais, he was ready, using it to extend his works further. Some have called his dances otherworldly or inhuman, some have seen similarities to the Bauhaus Theatre of the 1920s in Germany.

"Nik" was born in Southington, Connecticut, of Russian and German ancestry. The German modern dance had a definite influence on the young Nikolais. In 1933 he attended a performance by Mary Wigman and was so impressed with her use of percussion that he went to study with Truda Kaschmann, a former student of Wigman's. At the Bennington College summer sessions he came in contact with Hanya Holm, and after serving in the Army during World War II, he went to New York to study with her.

In 1948 he began the association with the Henry Street Playhouse on the Lower East Side of New York that provided him with a home base for over twenty years. In the early fifties he retired from performing to devote himself to choreography and teaching. Nikolais left the Henry Street Playhouse in 1970 and founded the Chimera Foundation for Dance and the Louis-Nikolais Dance Theatre Lab

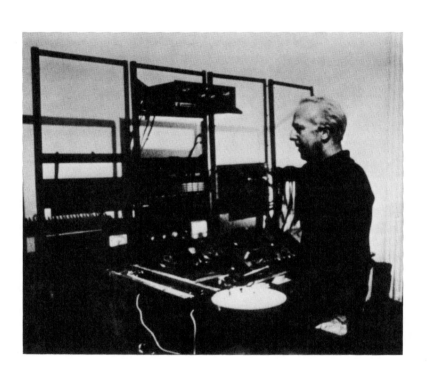

with Murray Louis, his associate and principal dancer since 1949. Nikolais' legacy lives through his pedagogy and the performance of his works by Murray Louis and Nikolais Dance, directed by Louis.

These excerpts from "Nik: A Documentary" contain the artistic philosophy of Alwin Nikolais.

It is abrasive to one's ego to be an esthetic revolutionary. A long time passes before language catches up with the germinal machineries of such a change. Consequently only peripheral descriptions are given into the archives of one's time, and any verbalization in depth is not guaranteed even at a later time. This is so in the temporal art of (dance) theater particularly.

In my own case, I look back with a sort of wonderment at the things I did—intuitively—in innocence—mixed, of course, with some indulgences and an occasional escapism. There were so many things that happened—profound and foolish, playful and diabolically real.

First came the annoyance with the self-expression rampant in the late 40s. The self as a sole germinal point of all value. It was as if an immaculate conception took place—as if one's presence was a self-induced miracle, and each gesture was a radiant gift bestowed upon the environment and whatever existed within it. There was little acknowledgement of external source of heritage. In most cases the stimuli derived from neurotic frictions. These were treasured as events of great import and merely reliving the situation was thought an act of choreographic merit. Behavior more worthy of clinical study than art was placed on stage in enthusiastic and somewhat orgiastic profusion.

I found myself realizing a new philosophy and consequently creating new techniques. Perhaps it was that I had the philosophy but had to clarify it to myself. I recognized the pattern of religious dynamics—particularly in the Christian belief where man, built in the image of a god, created a direct line of energy from that concept—there was an imagined spiritual umbilical cord nourishing him. In this fantasy he built moralities and laws. He built life on this basis and created art despite it.

It was Darwin who cut the cord. Man dangling like putty from a cord from heaven up above, flopped in the morass of primordial ooze. He did not realize that instead of being the embodiment of an ageless bewhiskered god, he was for the first time given not only a foot upon the earth, but a place within the sun—and more importantly, an entity—albeit a microscopic one—in the universe. Man's definition changed—his energy and life source were re-routed. His whole physical environment structured upon the basis of godliness—this pipeline to his god was severed and he had only himself.

If Darwin ruined man's concept of his divinity, Freud gave the final blow by exposing his uglies. With ties to god cut, now his self-expression had no parentage other than his personal itch. He turned his reverence to himself—uglies and all. Again art happened despite this. Man was now stuck with a sex-dominated libido. He was now man-god—self-important—inviolable—the thing from which all blessings flow.

With Einstein, again life dynamics changed. The circuitry again repatterned—but whereas before there were semi-permanent patterns, now the patterns changed to suit the venture. Man was permitted variable vistas.

Yet with a whole civilization system built upon the idea of proprietary rights not only of the flesh but land as well, a fixed point was an essential to life, like the tonality of the old Western musical system. There was always the "Do," and the sonata of living was always in accord and in reference to it. Perhaps the jump in divorce rates and Schoenberg's 12-tone system of music were not strange bedfellows. The itch to be flexible—to shift the "Do."

* * *

My total theater concept consciously started about 1950, although the seeds of it began much earlier I'm sure. First was expansion. I used masks and props—the masks, to have the dancer become something else; and props, to extend his physical size in space. (These latter were not instruments to be used as shovels or swords—but rather as extra bones and flesh.) I began to see the potentials of this new creature and in 1952

produced a program called *Masks Props & Mobiles*. I began to
establish my philosophy of man being a fellow traveler within
the total universal mechanism rather than the god from which
all things flowed. The idea was both humiliating and aggran-
dizing. He lost his domination but instead became kinsman to
the universe.

* * *

With the breakdown of story-line, choreographic structure
necessarily changed. With the further breakdown of physical
centralization—the lid was off. Logic of metronomic and sun
time was no longer necessary. Time no longer had to support
logical realistic events. It too could be decentralized but more
importantly, breaking the barrier of literal time throws the creator into visions and possible motional itineraries way beyond
the literal visions (particularly if physical emphasis is subdued).
The time-space canvas was now free. The ecology of the space
canvas now could be balanced—no dominant Aunt Minnie—
no nonreturnable bottles grinning out of the landscape. Now
we are permitted visions into the world in which we live and
perhaps even into the universe. We might even, then, return to
the vision of self but placed more humbly into the living landscape, adding grandeur to vision of self—not in proud pigeon
arabesques but as consonant members of the environment—
enriched by the resonance of that which surrounds us, a shared
energy interplaying with vital discussions rather than domi-
neering argument.

* * *

I was all for understanding the landscape of self by sensing
the presence of the sun and the ant within it. I hoped as well
to find the universe and the microbe—then I dared to smash
these boundaries to explore into the mystical blackness of pri-
malities—motion as an art—void of physical vision despite the
fact that physical vision was the means by which we perceived
the wondrous blackness. I don't mean to imply that all humanistic identifiable art was without dimension. Surely Martha had
wondrous blackness but it was always subservient to the figure.

What preposterous expectation—to ask a dancer to give up self-presence to expose motion—through him rather than on him.

* * *

Dancers often get into the pitfall of emotion rather than motion. To me motion is primary—it is the condition of motion which culminates into emotion. In other words it is our success or failure in action in time and space which culminates in emotion. This drama of action is universally understood by Chinese, Africans, South Americans and the Zulus. We do not have to be educated to understand the abstract language of motion, for motion is the stuff with which our every moment of life is preciously concerned. So in the final analysis the dancer is a specialist in the sensitivity to, the perception and the skilled execution of motion. Not movement but rather the qualified itinerary en route. The difference may be made even clearer by giving the example of two men walking from Hunter College to 42nd and Broadway. One man may accomplish it totally unaware of and imperceptive to the trip, having his mind solely on the arrival. He has simply moved from one location to another. The other may, bright-eyed and bright-brained, observe and sense all thru which he passes. He has more than moved—he is in motion.

* * *

I have often tried to trace my path of development. It has by no means been a clear-cut progress. The first chore was to drive—coerce—bludgeon—love and bribe the dancer to extricate himself from the patterns of self-clinical and cathartic indulgence and place him in skilled conversation with the environment and the things and happenings within it. Here I meant not just a presence in space—a place free of obstacles in which one could cavort, turn, kick legs, wrestle with fellow dancers. I meant much more than orientation.

I looked to space as a potential 3-dimensional canvas which even in the most simple terms allows and invites a sense of relationship. One's realized presence within space creates an acoustical sounding board even before the dynamics of action takes place. But—how difficult to teach the performer that presence alone in this instance is insufficient. How to teach the dancer to make himself right in any part of a space structure by acknowledging with his body the proportions and dynamic vitality of that relationship—just as a painter can qualify a line anywhere on the canvas by virtue of its position and structure—and make it beautiful.

Now when the dancer by his action creates other linear boundaries or volumes of space these also are made visible and alive by the textural behaviorism of his body—all of this taking intense realization and concentration of the dancer upon the spatial involvements. If he cannot do this—the involvements will be dead—without audibility—they remain unspoken—in reality—unperformed. The relationships exist only as symbols—unexplained.

Let's take the space environment as I outlined above and qualify it further by the presence of another dancer or several dancers—all alive and responsive to the spatial behaviorism as it is activated by their orchestral involvement with it and each other. Suppose we think of time and shape in the same terms— not involved in the drama of boy meets girl—nor even in humanistic presence—but rather as dynamic musicalities of action of fabulously sensitive instruments, reminding one of things beyond the physicalities of the instruments—yet seen through them. Abstract expressionism? Perhaps—but basic dance—relieved of the romantic fallacy of the inviolability of a dull fat arse (or a puny skinny one—for that matter). Here our identification is with the rumblings and utterings and songs of generative primal stuffs—the stuffs which disclose and qualify not only the dimension of nature—to which man belongs— but of man as well. Dehumanization?

From the point of view of mathematics, dynamics, dispersion of visual and auditory events and energies I caused the whole upset to dance dynamics. Whatever anyone else might have done or still is doing within that or this period of so-called avant-garde dance theater, this particular creative vision seems to be peculiarly my own—and is still often misinterpreted and mostly unexamined in terms of its basic social and esthetic germination. Most interpretations still evolve around the Nureyev principle and the brother-in-spirit identifications with humanistic events on stage no matter how abstractly whacky the dance gesture might be. It's still Nureyev or Fonteyn doing it. Bare-assed or dressed—frontal or back-al—jeans or tutus—whiskers or wigs. Of course the specialists are bewildered. Reminds me of a shoe store man in Hartford. He often stood outside his shop. When I passed he never said "Hello" to me—it was always to my shoes.

* * *

I consider myself to be somewhat of a greybeard not far from half a century in the "business." There are simple mathematical facts in such a lengthy and deeply saturated involvement. It is impossible to survive that length of time in an art without accomplishment, a sense of humor, and I'm inclined to add, a certain attraction, innocently or otherwise, towards vulgarity. This is aside, of course, from the hysterical search for beauty. During the course of this adventure, one measures himself against a million things, incidents, experiences, involvements. One takes one's esthetic temperature 10 billion times— always curious, always questioning and most always doubtful, at least on the surface.

Behind it all there develops an inward assurance—fortified over the years as one tests oneself—first upon relatives and friends—next upon cities of people, then upon nations and then the world. Historical presence, social dynamics and fortuitous timing can cause storms, sometimes swamping your craft and other times lifting it on wind-wings.

Your welfare is greatly a matter of whether your esthetic vision coincides with the whims of history in progress. Even the weather matters. At this time I am back in the U.S. one month following a 4-month tour of Europe, the Near East and a bit of Africa. It was a glorious magic carpet tour. Paris, Lisbon, Vienna and Teheran were ecstatic. Seven thousand each night in the 3rd-century Roman theater in Carthage thrilled us no end. Playing on top of the old walls in Dubrovnik and the ancient Diocletian palace in Split added more glamour. But London! Carolyn [Carlson] was ill and had left the tour. The company was a wreck—tour tired. Our tech people got involved in some misunderstandings, causing an hysterical delay in set-up—even holding the audience until we were technically ready. A heat wave hit London and no air conditioning, not even good ventilation in the theater—and to top it off we were booked at the tail end of an oversaturated dance season to which the Londoners responded halfheartedly. That we survived the 3-week season at all was a miracle. Obviously critical response in London—although good—was not anywhere nearly as fine as Vienna or Paris. The works, of course, were the same. Now had we not had brilliant receptions in so many other places one would begin to question validities. Then one begins to think of the British as people. Is their esthetic Rorschach as good as the French or Viennese? Then I remembered the hysterically ecstatic reception 2 years earlier in London. This time the Londoners complained about missing Murray and Phyllis Lamhut too—and I thought Oh Gawd—it's the Nureyev syndrome again and I was angry.

Then there was the difference in reception to different pieces. The French loved *Echo*—the British were somewhat indifferent. Some pieces are apt to vary in different countries. (I avoid my humorous pieces in Italy because the Italians do not respond to them at all.)

Anyway—in just this one instance you can see that it is essential for the artist to fortify himself against such experiences and to have great knowledge and sense of value for his own work. It is not ego or immodesty, it is simply an inner and necessary assurance gained in a vast number of experiences and over a very long time. At this point in a career it is almost impossible to make the wrong stroke upon the canvas. It is mathematically unreasonable. And if the artist does make the mistake he certainly will see it and will not exhibit the canvas.

BACK TO BASICS

Paul Taylor
1930–

With almost no dance training and already in his early twenties, Paul Taylor stepped onto the stage at the American Dance Festival and into the dance world in 1952. He eventually gravitated toward Martha Graham, performing in her company for what he calls "six wonderful, hideous, bewitching, boring, tickling, vivid years." During that same period, he experimented with his own choreography, presenting his first full-fledged concert in 1957.

By that time, Taylor had already shown his work in concerts shared with other choreographers. He analyzed those early dances and concluded that they "seemed nice, but not nice enough." Taylor asked himself questions about style, structure, point of view. His quest for answers led him, in essence, to the same path the modern dance had traveled— discarding everything he had experienced in the past and starting fresh with his own explorations. "Back to Basics," excerpted from Taylor's 1987 autobiography Private Domain, offers insights into this process which gained the choreographer instant notoriety and launched his independent career.

In 1961, Taylor officially broke from Graham's company and launched his own with a tour of Italy. Since then, he has continued to mine his choreographic impulses, born from what he describes as "pure hues, true silences, perfect vacuums." Taylor did return to a "more kinetic approach," as he suggests in this article, developing a style known for its strong physicality and great movement invention. The results include such diverse works as Aureole (1962), Big Bertha (1970), Esplanade (1975), Speaking in Tongues (1988), and Company B (1991).

Everywhere the city's inhabitants are on the move—objects just waiting to be found, make-dos of an untraditionalized piebald nation, milling and walking, sitting in vehicles or on benches, tearing off after a bus, some drunk and lying flat out. Lines of restless people at banks, theaters, and rest rooms. Wads crammed into elevators or spaced artistically on subway platforms or leaning against skyscrapers. They are standing, squatting, sitting everywhere like marvelous ants or bees, and their moves and stillnesses are ABCs that if given a proper format could define dance in a new way. All is there for the taking. There's no need to invent exotic climes or bucolic Edens. An array of riches surrounded me daily, and its timeless beauty needed to be pointed out and shared.

To begin, I amass a collection of natural postures, stick-figure drawings which fall naturally into five stacks—ones of legs standing, squatting, and kneeling and two other categories of arm and head positions. (Later on, I run across an article on posture in *Scientific American* in which the author has made similar groupings.) Because my fridge is empty, my collection is stored there. Each category is then pared down to representative examples and strung together. Like in butterfly collecting, the idea is to net the best beauts for scrutiny. Epic, a twenty-minute solo, is to be the first section of a full-evening work titled *7 New Dances.*

There is also the matter of music to redefine. If dance could be broadened to include everyday moves, so could its accompaniment. I choose the sounds of heartbeats, wind, rain, a complicated collage of background noise, plus two compositions by John Cage, one of which he writes for me to be played on quasi-musical instruments (a pan, a radio, and a piano lid). Besides myself, the dancers are Donya Feuer, Toby Armour, and Cynthia Stone—well-trained professionals whose past accomplishments give them the right to toss their technique out the window. Bob [Robert Rauschenberg] suggests that the costumes be our own everyday clothes, and that the set for one of the dance's sections be a live dog sitting on a mat.

Much of the eight months of rehearsals—mostly at night, since we all work during the day—is spent unlearning dancer-ly habits, because the natural movements, when done in a dancy way, look unnatural, and so we have to find a new, yet equally stylized, way to do them. We memorize vast amounts of uneven counts in order to give rhythmic variety and to keep from falling into monotony. Learning these counts is like memorizing a page of numbers in a phone book. It also takes a lot of time to learn exactly how, and with which dynamic, each move is to be performed. For instance, the light turn of a head, the heavy drop of an akimbo arm, the slowing down of a run into a walk. When done right, there is much appeal to the tilting of Toby's shoulders as she stands with her weight on one leg, and the soft settling of Cynthia's arms as she folds them, and the way that the pointy heel of Donya's shoe digs into the floor as she lifts her toes—also, when the girls gaze downwards, the lovely arching of their necks.

We find that each posture tends to get blurred when executed consecutively, and so it's necessary to surround each with stillness. The sequences take little physical exertion, make it impossible to rely on our muscle memories, and are difficult to remember. By isolating the postures in stillness, we are left with no chains of uninterrupted movement. There are few chances to use our muscles, and our brains are forced to spin through a good deal of mental gymnastics. Discovering how to hold still and yet remain active in a way that looks vital is the most difficult of all. The stillnesses are important and are to be on a par with the moves—as important as the negative space in paintings, the yin of the yang—as important as, if not more so than, silences in music. For dancers whose training has been in movement, this is like a springtail losing its tail, or a snail losing its pace. Many of the rehearsals are devoted to nothing but holding still.

The walking, running, and isolated postures are built into what's intended to be a formal, objective, practically scientific format. Surprisingly, much of it turns out as if it were saying something dramatic. For example, in *Events I,* when Toby and Donya are spaced near to each other, their long series of shifting postures seems to indicate a restless sort of waiting, as if something dire is about to occur; and then when Donya final-

ly walks away, she is not merely moving to a different spot—
she is *leaving* Toby. The sound of wind adds to the tension, and
an emotional relationship between the two girls seems to have
built up, then dispersed on Donya's departure.

With no dance steps for us to hide behind, even more than
is usual the sequences are revealing us as people. Undisguised,
our individual traits are laid bare, and our shapes, spacings, and
timings are establishing definite emotional climates in all that
we do. In context, what was meant to be "scientific" has turned
out to be dramatic. Posture has become gesture. It is surprising
to find the two so closely related, in fact inseparable. I'd intended to present posture pictorially and uncolored by emotional
connotations, but I'm now forced to accept that the piece contains not only a collection of "facts" but the inescapable body
language inherent in all types of dance. Abstract and representational elements are battling with each other—an age-old situation that always makes arbiters out of choreographers.

By careful allotment of income, I've been able to rent the
Kaufmann Concert Hall of the 92nd Street YM-YWHA,
where my company of three and I are to show *7 New Dances*
on October 20, 1957. A few days before the concert I'm making a twenty-minute tape of the phone lady who announces
the time every ten seconds: "At the tone the time will be. . ."
I've decided that her spiel is supposed to match the exact time
during the concert when I'll be performing *Epic.* The phone
automatically cuts off every minute or so, causing a lot of
tedious retaping and splicing, also a skyrocketing phone bill.
I'm beginning to wonder if all the eight months of rehearsals
will be worth it, and it dawns on me that I've been so involved
with investigating the exciting realm of natural movement that
it hasn't occurred to me to imagine how the audience might
react. It's a chilling thought. The dance is pretty stark, certainly
less flashy than flipflops. Maybe folks won't go for this sort of
thing. But I shove the notion aside—aren't the girls and I
proven technicians who've earned the right to scrap dancy
dancing if we want to?

The program begins and I'm standing there under Tharon
Musser's lighting in a freshly ironed suit that I haven't worn

since coming to New York. The phone lady is making her announcements and I'm remembering the tricky counts and executing interesting street gleanings, but, sooner than I would've guessed, a few of the audience rise from their front seats and head up the aisle. I conclude that the correct time must have reminded them that they had to be somewhere. Even so, I'm becoming more unsure about *Epic's* ability to establish and sustain interest. Each slow ten-second interval is passing excruciatingly. Several more people leave at a polite but firm pace; then others accumulate into a solid mass and practically canter up the aisles. Inwardly, I'm sinking; outwardly, tics of my neck are betraying nervousness. By the time the solo is over, the hall has been emptied of all but a small handful of stalwart friends, friends who are able to enjoy my embarrassments best.

The solo over, I go offstage and tell the girls not to expect a large house.

After *Events I,* performed without further events out front, I do *Resemblance,* the item with the dog as its set. The dog's name is Duchess, and she's a mongrel rented from Animal Talent Scouts in the Village. When Bob saw a llama there, he asked for it instead, but it was too expensive. Although inexpensive, Duchess is the only one of us who is being paid and has a no-biting clause in her contract. At the dress rehearsal she reacted poorly to the moment when pianist David Tudor banged down the piano lid. She then raced to the basement, barking hysterically, and her trainer had to give her a tranquilizer. Now, as I'm performing my walking dance, she is poised on her mat, half-risen, staring at the piano worriedly, whites of eyes glistening and ears laid back. She is usurping all of the audience's attention. I'm sensing that I may as well not be there. Then, tail curled under, Duchess starts creeping offstage. Her trainer's finger appears from behind a drape, sending her back, but she attempts to exit again and again, each time being reprimanded. Her intelligent legs are fighting with her valiant heart. Instead of being a disciplined stage set, she's letting unprofessionalism get the better of her and ruining my dance. I'm thinking never to let a dog upstage me again, and that if Bob should ever suggest anything live, even his stuffed angora goat with a tire around it, it will be the end of our beautiful collaborations.

And now the girls do *Panorama*. My studio mirrors are the set. These are to remind the audience that what they are seeing is a reflection of the postures that they themselves hold in real life, but since there's almost nobody in the hall, the mirrors are reflecting empty seats and probably not reminding anybody of anything.

The concert continues with Toby and me in *Duet*. This dance is to feature nothingness taken to its ultimate. Before the curtain goes up, she sits on the stage and I stand close by. We start looking calm in an exciting way. The curtain lifts, exactly four minutes pass, and then it comes down. Not having batted an eyelid, or moved anything at all, we feel moderately satisfied and go prepare for our next item. This time everything has come off perfectly. It's been the limit.

Then we all perform the finale—rather minimal, but like fireworks in contrast to Duet—*Opportunity,* and immediately following it I go to my dressing room, where the manager of the concert hall has been waiting to inform me that if I should ever rent the theater again, it will be over his dead body.

A few weeks later Louis Horst's review comes out in *Dance Observer*. It consists of four square inches of blank space with the initials LH at the bottom. My first reaction is outrage. The review wasn't even very long. And then I realize that my own worst suspicions have been confirmed. Folks have indeed misinterpreted my beautiful ABCs of posture as being a nightmare alphabet. Other reviewers, all except friend David Vaughan, are very stern. Even the usually forbearing Walter Terry headlines his article with "Experiment? Joke? War of nerves?," then accuses me of trying to drive him insane. *New York Times* critic John Martin, one of the first to go up the aisle, predicts in a Sunday column that the Horst review is to become a collector's item. It's been an ignoble fall, and in the months that follow, teachers, fellow students, and dancer friends regard me suspiciously with sideways glances. Martha shakes her gnarled finger and accuses me of being a "naughty boy."

Yet there are certain benefits. I've more or less defined for myself some roots to work from. The relationship between posture and its pal gesture has become clear and might be something that can be applied to dance steps. By failing to find a completely objective approach, and by failing to disguise the dancer's individual body language, my awareness of the communicability of dance has increased. By assuming that dance could be anything one wanted it to be, I lost an audience, but this tells me to bear them in mind next time I try to communicate private dreams. And then there is what no amount of paid advertising could have brought—immediate notoriety. Almost everyone in the New York dance community has now heard my name. Having accomplished more than what I set out to do, I decide to get back to a more kinetic approach, and dive into new dances with a vengeance. I won't get mad, I'll get even.

IT'S ABOUT DANCE

Alvin Ailey
1951–1989

Born in Rogers, Texas, Alvin Ailey was introduced to dance by performances of the Katherine Dunham Company and the Ballet Russe. His formal dance training began in Los Angeles with an introduction to Lester Horton's classes by his life-long friend, Carmen de Lavallade.

By 1958, Ailey had moved to New York City and performed in various shows including House of Flowers and Sing, Man, Sing. But he saw few opportunities for himself in the modern dance world. In his book Revelations: The Autobiography of Alvin Ailey (with A. Peter Bailey), Ailey writes, . . . "[T]here were many terrific black dancers in New York City, and yet, except for an occasional concert or art show, there was no place for them to dance. . . There was practically no way for us to fulfill our compelling desire to participate fully in the dance world. There was no Lester Horton on the East Coast dance scene. Even against those long odds, I very much wanted to be a choreographer. . . . I had my own ideas, and the time had come for me to make my own decisions." Ailey began by creating Blues Suite, a dance about the Dew Drop Inn from his childhood, filled with the sounds of "funky blues music," and Revelations, drawn from "blood memories" of the "very theatrical, very intense" Texas churches of his youth.

Alvin Ailey went on to create his internationally renowned Alvin Ailey American Dance Theater, choreograph 150 ballets, and receive such prestigious awards as the Dance Magazine Award and the Kennedy Center Award. But the racism experienced as a child gnawed at him his entire life. In "It's About Dance" excerpted from his autobiography, Ailey explains how his response to racism influenced his own company.

I am very fond of dancers. I like their personalities, I like who they are—their spirit, their physicality, their creativity, their yearning to be perfect. I look for dancers who have something unusual about them physically—a special turn of the leg, a special stretch of the back. I look for dancers who have rubato in their bodies. I believe that dance is not what you do from one movement to the next, it's what happens in between those two movements with the body. I look for dancers who have an oozy quality in their movement. I like dancers who are temperamental, who are expressive, who show their feelings, who are open and out, not hidden, who want to show themselves to the audience. I like personalities, not cookie-cutter dancers—a row of this, a row of that. That's what I accuse Balanchine of: making everyone who dances for him blank-faced.

Dancers these days must also have technique—classical, modern, and jazz. My earlier dancers were not the world's greatest technicians. None of those girls were about to turn forty-two fouettés on a dime, but they had a funk; they had a stride; they had history; they had a menace about them that the young kids don't have today. Today's kids are very technical. They can do eighteen pirouettes on a dime and get their leg way above the head and hold it there. But the insight is not the same: It's not as giving, not as warm. They need to give themselves to the dance, to project themselves from the inside out. That's what we get after them about.

We coach and direct them to bring out their personalities. We *want* them to be capable of acting out various parts, to become the different individuals in each ballet. That's where personality comes in. It even took talented dancers like Judy Jamison and Donna Wood time and practice to become secure enough physically to let go and truly be themselves. But when you suddenly find yourself in contact with the audience and it can take years—the result is extraordinary. I saw that happen with Judy; she didn't come on in an extraordinary way with audiences until *Cry.* Her shyness hurt her, but with *Cry* she became herself. Once she found this contact, this release, she poured her being into everybody who came to see her perform. She grew to another level, went on to Broadway, and now has her own dance company.

The question of dance and race is an ever-present one. Look at the problem in England right now. There are black dancers in the Royal Ballet School, but the RBS doesn't want them, so as a result the really good black dancers with potential are sent to Arthur Mitchell's school. The Royal Ballet has an arrangement with Arthur to take them and nurture them so they don't have to deal with all those young black artists. You still don't see many black dancers in classical companies. The Europeans are more open than the Americans. (Maurice Béjart [then Director of Dance at the Théâtre Royal de la Monnaie in Brussels] has three black dancers, for example.) In American companies, though, there is still an overlay of racism. I remember in 1966 when my company was going through one of its periodic dissolutions, some of our very top, fantastic dancers—Judith Jamison, Morton Winston, and Miguel Godreau—were invited to the Harkness Ballet. All had terrible times; when it came to utilizing their fantastic abilities, Harkness simply didn't have a clue.

Here, in short, is the big problem with white ballet companies: Does one really want to see a black swan among thirty-two swans in *Swan Lake* or a black peasant girl in *Giselle?* It's historically inaccurate, is the line taken by many of those in charge. Agnes de Mille used that argument with black dancers, and I'll never forgive her for it. When she was holding auditions for a Texas musical, *Ninety Degrees in the Shade,* I believe, she told the black dancers who came to the audition that they were historically inappropriate and refused to hire them.

I give no credence to that position whatsoever. What we're talking about here is dance. We're talking about fantasy, not reality. We're in the theater, not in a history seminar. It's the same as saying that Japanese dancers can't dance the blues—well, they do in *my* company. Japanese dancers understand the blues as well as anybody. When I began using them and some white dancers in *Blues Suite* and *Revelations,* I got flack from some black groups who resented it. They felt anyone not black was out of place. I received many letters in protest. My answer was that their presence universalizes the material. . . .

It goes back to Lester Horton, who was an influence on me in so many ways. When I was with him, he was very involved with the Japanese community in Los Angeles and had a couple of Japanese dancers. I believe there's something in the Japanese aesthetic that is totally black. The Buddhism and zen that they practice in Japan, and teach their children, is very close to what we have in Bible school in the black church. It's about humanism, respect, and loving people.

Part Four

THE
NEW REBELS

INTRODUCTION

By the 1960s, technical proficiency had become an end in itself for modern dancers, rather than the means to an end. Technique became set and strict, codified in the style of the originator, with emphasis on greater and greater achievement. Only those teaching in the Laban-Wigman-Holm tradition included improvisation in their classes. Aspects of ballet were incorporated increasingly into modern dance classes, ballet barres were installed in modern dance studios, and many modern dancers took ballet classes regularly. Thus the wide philosophical gap between the two dance forms began to narrow.

In 1962 a new rebellion came which was the most far-reaching to date. This was the Judson Dance Theater, the first co-operative effort within modern dance since the Workers Dance League. The Judson group began with the composition students of Robert Dunn, a musician who had worked with Graham and Cunningham. Most of the students were from the Cunningham studio and company. One of them had studied with Anna Halprin, an avant-garde dancer on the West Coast who worked in improvisation (some of the others studied with her a few years later). The Judson Dance Theater, therefore, evolved from the existing avant-garde, extending their mentors' revolutionary theories farther than ever. This newest rebellion was against the established modern dance: their mentors' mentors.

The founding dancers included Trisha Brown, Judith Dunn, David Gordon, Deborah and Alex Hay, Steve Paxton, Yvonne Rainer, and James Waring. A place to perform was provided at the Judson Memorial Church in New York City by Al Carmines, associate minister and director of the arts program of the church. The first performance was held in the church gymnasium with borrowed technical equipment; later the performances were moved upstairs to the church sanctuary. All decisions affecting the group were made collectively. These dancers were not interested in repertory, the proscenium stage, or technique. They were interested in individual creativity.

People came to their performances, including a dancer who had tried to work with Paul Taylor and studied with Merce Cunningham—Twyla Tharp. Trying desperately to find a toehold in dance-making, she recalled Ruth St. Denis's advice to Martha Graham to "go out and get" a dance. Tharp's seven-minute choreographic debut took place in 1965.

At the same time the Judson Dance Theater began to take shape, other dancers and choreographers were erasing the dividing lines between modern dance and ballet. Ballet companies began to introduce into their repertory works that had been choreographed by modern dancers. One of the first such crossovers was the New York City Ballet's performance of Merce Cunningham's *Summerspace* as originally done by the Cunningham Company, with the addition of toe shoes for the ballerinas. Ironically, this occurred just when Cunningham's influence on the Judson group was greatest. Later, other ballet companies, such as the Joffrey Ballet, the American Ballet Theatre, the Cincinnati Ballet, and the Hartford Ballet, added to their repertory works by José Limón, Lester Horton, and Twyla Tharp. The Connecticut College summer program became the American Dance Festival, which offered ballet and ethnic dance as well as modern dance. In 1978 the program moved again, this time to Duke University.

Meanwhile, the names of Clive Barnes, Marcia Siegel, Jill Johnston, Deborah Jowitt, Don McDonagh, Joseph Mazo, Anna Kisselgoff, Arlene Croce, and Walter Sorrell were added to the ranks of the critics. The tradition of dance books written by critics continued, with a substantial amount of literature on dance coming from these writers.

Another important development of the mid-sixties grew out of the political climate in America. Concurrent with the broadening of human rights for African-American people, African-American choreographers began to create dances that existed as works of art rather than as works of ethnic art. The dances were based on ethnic themes only at the will of the choreographers. Their predecessors, such as Pearl Primus, Katherine

Dunham, and Geoffrey Holder, had been limited entirely to African, Afro-Caribbean, and Afro-American themes. The new African-American dancers—Alvin Ailey, Donald McKayle, Rod Rodgers, Eleo Pomare, Raymond Johnson, Gus Solomons Jr., and others—choreographed dances on a wide range of subject matter for their companies.

The "Happenings" of the late sixties, which were an outgrowth of the Judson movement, seem in retrospect to have been a barometer for the temper of the young Americans at that time. Individualism was encouraged, but individuals banded together more cohesively than before. Some of the major pop art painters and sculptors, such as Robert Rauschenberg and Robert Morris, began to choreograph. Audience participation became standard. The emphasis of the Happenings was on spontaneous improvisation, natural movement, nonmovement, nondancers, nudity, street or secondhand clothes (noncostume), and the use of ordinary objects. Performances were often given in lofts, but were just as often given any place, any time.

The far-out went as far as it could—performing in fountains, in plazas and museums, and eventually on rooftops and on walls.

Although the outward appearance differed from the dance of Isadora, the spirit of the movement, in its rejection of all dance that is not natural, was hers.

THE PROCESS
IS THE
PURPOSE

Anna Halprin
1920–

*B*y the early 1960s, Anna Halprin had already influenced some
dancers who later became key figures in the Judson Dance
Theater. She worked with improvisation, using a complete
range of movement, and often performed outside the theater.

A native of Winnetka, Illinois, Halprin studied at the University of
Wisconsin with Margaret H'Doubler. After graduation, she made her
debut in the 1944 Broadway musical Sing Out Sweet Land, *choreographed by Doris Humphrey and Charles Weidman. She married
environmental architect Lawrence Halprin, and they moved to
California, where she developed all of her work.*

Anna Halprin founded the Dancers' Workshop in 1955, a collaborative interdisciplinary performance group, and Tamalpa Institute in
1978, a center for expressive arts education. Her work developed to
include an exploration of pertinent social issues, and dance as a healing art. A cancer survivor since 1978, Halprin is now concerned with
healing in the context of the person, the group, and on a global level.
She has written several books, including Moving Toward Life, Five
Decades of Transformational Dance, *an inspiring compendium of
essays, scores and stories.*

This interview is an early conversation, from the late 60s, about the
methodology and theories which Halprin has developed over her more-
than-fifty-year long career.

An Interview by Vera Maletic

Maletic. It seems to me that your personal approach to movement has evolved from some specific needs of our contemporary life, particularly in the U.S.A. and [on] the West Coast. What do you aim for with your educational and performance activities in relation to the trainees and in relation to the audience?

Halprin. Of course, this is not the easiest question to answer. It's like asking what your whole life is about. But I think I can start with the first notion that comes into my head, and that is I have developed an enormous concern and interest in movement as it relates to a more natural outgrowth of expression. In other words, I am disinterested in movement so highly stylized that we must say this is a Dancer. Anybody's a dancer to me at any time when I am involved in communicating with that person through his movement. This has led me to a way of working with students that does not rely so much on traditional or conventional means, which tend to make the kind of dancer that I'm really interested in for myself.

More and more I have begun to stress breathing as a base, because I find that the deeper the student can get into the breathing center, the more open she becomes to releasing areas in her body which become alive and accessible to her for her work. So this is a very important base of our work. You know, my training has been with Margaret H'Doubler from Wisconsin University. Of course she was always interested in movement as an expressive medium for communication and was never interested in imposed style and patterns of movement. In a very convincing way she grounded me in a more biological approach to movement—movement that is more natural to the nervous system, to the bone structure, to the muscle action. I found that in my training with her, the stress in movement was on understanding your body as action and, at the same time, being able to appreciate feedback, so that the relationship of the feeling to the movement was complete. Now when you learn imposed patterned movement, you're so involved in learning the pattern that the tendency is simply to cut off the feeling aspect. And by feeling, I'm not referring to a kind of free-style self-expression. I mean just the feeling that's inherent when you clench your fist in anger, or stamp your feet, or jump in exhilaration. These are all natural and the most expressive movement we do. And when you become aware of the movement and the feeling it's evoking, you begin to have the freedom to use it consciously and excitingly, and that's when you begin to become an artist in your material.

It's that approach to movement that I'm talking about. I've never taught classes in which I teach a style, or a pattern, or set progression. First of all, I keep changing from year to year. I keep finding new things that I keep incorporating. Recently I've gotten very involved in developing a new use of body training through principles that have to do with getting the body into positions of stress. And then—it's almost like isometric exercises—from the stress position it goes into a trembling that gets you into a kind of forced breathing. It must change the chemistry in the body, because it's as if your whole circulatory system just comes alive. This is something very new to me, because I've never been able to get at the circulatory system before. I'll show you some of the movements afterwards, if you'd like to see them. The efficiency is just incredible. By placing your body in a position, you get all the strength and a fantastic sense of your body as a totality. So we've been experimenting, as we constantly do, with new methods to get deeper and deeper into the body itself.

Maletic. I think you have answered my second question already. It was: how would you define your approach to education, art, and theatre, apart from traditional concepts?

Halprin. Well, I think this goes back to the way I have always related myself to dance and life. That is, I try not to separate the experiences of life, because we are in confrontation with our experiences, constantly, in art. And this brings me to an appreciation of, or an emphasis on, the relationship between personal growth and artistic growth. For the two must go hand in hand; otherwise there is no maturity that ever takes place. Since I've been working simultaneously in education and theatre all my life, it's hard for me to know the source for an idea. But I do know that in the theatre experiences, I want very much to deal with people on that stage who are identifying with very real experiences in life, in such a way that the audiences can identify themselves with the so-called performers. Rather than just looking at somebody doing something very unusual, I want the audience to be able to identify and realize that this is a person more than he is a dancer, a person who identifies with very real things.

We don't even accept the theatre as a conventional place where the audience is here and you're there, but it *is* a place, and whatever you do in that place is valid because it's the place. You don't have to be on the stage separating here from there. This desire to merge a very life-like situation into the concept of the dance is very true also in my training. Everything we do in dance somehow or other usually relates to who you are as a person, and this affects how you see things and feel things and relate to people. Again, it's this nonseparation of life and art, so that somehow or other it becomes a heightening process.

Maletic. Do you feel there is a difference between self-exploration or self-expression as individual therapeutic experience and as an artistic expression?

Halprin. This is a hard question to answer right now, because the word therapy is being used by so many different people in so many different ways. So is the word creativity. At one time, you could use the word creativity and feel fairly safe, but now there's creative merchandise. Everything's creative—you can get a creative ice cream cone. The word therapy is beginning to become like a tea party. You know, let's get together and have a little therapy session. So it gets a little difficult. But I would say that if you use the word therapy in terms of personal growth, any art experience that is valid to a person and that is based on personal experience certainly, automatically, must have therapeutic value. But if your attention as an artist is only on what you are getting therapeutically, you are not paying attention to the fact that essentially you're a craftsman, that essentially your job is to be a vehicle for other people.

To me, a performer is simply a vehicle, a submergence of the ego. Otherwise, you may as well stay in your studio. But when you take the responsibility for performing for an audience, you are then accepting the fact that you must go through some sort of distilling process in which the personal experience has become so zeroed and so heightened by a clarity that you know exactly what you're dealing with. You have so much skill that you can get right down to the essence. Then you find the movement—spatial, dynamic—essence of that idea inherent not only in how your body moves, but in an awareness of where you are in space, an awareness of the total thing. That has therapeutic value—that's OK—but that shouldn't be your concern.

Maletic. What is your criterion for determining whether a performance is true or genuine in involvement and feeling, or whether it is a phony? Also, what is your criterion for determining the choice of events for a public theatre performance?

Halprin. We're in such a violent, explosive period of experimentation. At least I am, and certainly all the young artists I work with. Yet I know that before I ever present a work in public, I've gone through two years' research, two years of going through many, many sketches. And I work very hard to have a score which externalizes the elements so I can get further and further detached from the source, so I can be detached from it and still be very much involved. Other than that, I don't know how to make any judgment about other people's work. First of all, being here on the West Coast, I don't see an awful lot, and what I have seen coming on tour is working in such a different direction from mine. It's hard to know. But because I've spent so many years in movement, I can, just intuitively, tell when a performance is lacking in what I call the audience dimension. And I usually can tell on the basis that the experience just hasn't been structured at all, that the individual is behaving, not moving. There's a difference.

Maletic. What are the concepts of your kinetic theatre?

Halprin. The theatre is based on the human expression which comes primarily from movement, from motion. But it goes into the other areas of human expression, which include the visual and the speaking and all of the things that represent a total kind of experience. And this is what I am most interested in developing, a theatre which uses the total resources of the human being. So, rather than call it dance, which seems always to be limited, I'd rather find a new word right now. Although it's basically what dance was in its more primitive time.

Maletic. Of the main streams in psychology, Jungian, Gestalt, Existential, etc., which do you feel the closest affinity with?

Halprin. I feel most closely aligned with the Gestalt therapy, but that may be because of my contact with Fritz Perls. When I read his book, *Gestalt Therapy,* or when I work with him, I'm continually reminded of similarities. It's the coming together of all the parts. That is important to me, and it seems this is what is stressed in the Gestalt. I feel very identified with it.

Maletic. Have you had any psychedelic experiences and, if so, have they influenced your creativity?

Halprin. Yes, I have had a psychedelic experience, only once, and it did get me in touch with a very deep breathing experience in which I was able to sense what the Chinese call the red spot. I was able to start the radiation all through my body, and this relaxation that set in was so profound, it completely changed my body structure. This happened at the University of California. Somebody was filming it. Afterwards, I felt very different in posture and alignment, and when I started to move I felt very different. But when I saw the film, I didn't even recognize myself. My body went into a very effortless type of alignment, and my movements had no effort. Without getting out of breath I was able to move with so much more strength and richness. I felt so much more alive. Because I was able to direct it towards the discovery of relaxation through breathing, the experience had very illuminating effects.

Maletic. Could you tell me something about your professional background and the persons who influenced you?

Halprin. I have been dancing ever since I was a little girl, in a very free and natural way. When I went to college, I studied with Margaret H'Doubler. I would say that she was my great teacher. The more I work on my own, the more I keep coming back and saying, oh, this is what she meant, of course. Even though I have gone into a slightly different emphasis, I still feel I'm her student and I'm still learning. She's such a wealth of ideas, it's taken me years to accumulate the information that substantiates what she was saying. My husband has been very much a teacher for me because of his work in landscape architecture. He's made me

enormously aware of the choreography of space. A very important teacher in my life was Rabbi Kadushin, who made me very
aware of philosophical concepts in Judaism which reinforced my
belief in creativity as a means of strengthening a sense of self-
affirmation, not only to oneself, but to the many layers penetrat-
ing from oneself to others. This certainly developed a desire for,
and a belief in, human encounter on a creative level.

Maletic. Since I come from Europe, I wonder if you can tell
me if there are particular needs in this part of America which
create your kind of work. Is this kind of activity specific to the
West Coast?

Halprin. I suppose I again may sound a little biological, but I
think that the word is ecology and I think that there is something so vital about our natural surroundings that we have
become, perhaps unconsciously. . . . How can you live in this
kind of landscape, with the ocean, with the cliffs, with the vital
forces of nature at your feet all the time, and not be affected by
the so called nature-oriented point of view? You become vitally concerned with the materials, the sensual materials of our
lives, and with the almost primitive naiveness of being an extension of your environment. This begins to free you to appreciate
the very characteristics of what a human being is, and from there
you start coming out again. And when you start coming out and
relaxing, you are working in a sort of nonintellectual way.

I'll speak for myself. I have a tremendous faith in the process
of a human mechanism, and in creativity as an essential attribute
of all human beings. This creativity is stimulated only when the
sense organs are brought to life. This faith in the process is the
only goal or purpose I need. What happens as a result creates and
generates its own purpose. So I don't question the purpose
beforehand; I've already accepted the process as the purpose. In
this sense it's nonintellectual. I don't get all sorts of intellectual
theories that this dance work or this new piece in this blah blah
blah, but this is where we are in our growth, this is where we are
in our educational commitment. The process is the purpose; let
it be, let it keep growing, and something will happen. And what
happens generates it's own purpose. I'm being very repetitive,
but in this sense it's nonintellectual and very nature-oriented.

WE DON'T
TALK ABOUT IT.
WE ENGAGE IN IT.

Judith Dunn
1933–1983

*J*udith Dunn earned a Master's Degree in dance from Sarah
Lawrence College and taught for three years at Brandeis
University before becoming a member of the Merce Cunningham
Dance Company. She performed with Cunningham from 1958 to
1963 and was one of the original members of the Judson Dance
Theater. She then collaborated and toured with musician-composer Bill
Dixon. Ms. Dunn joined the faculty of Bennington College, where she
worked until 1977, when a brain tumor forced her to retire.

Artists for the most part don't think abstractly about communication. We study it. We engage in it. When asked, "Well, aren't
you interested in communicating?" I usually answer that I don't
think about it. This answer is almost always misunderstood.

I think about my work and the problems I have, both artistic and economic, getting it accomplished. I think about the
position of artists in our society, why it is that way and how I
am going to keep surviving as a practicing artist. I think about
the ideas and energy I have for work, and how only a fraction
of these plans will ever be realized. I think about artistic
endeavor being as essential as science for life. I think about art
processes and products as I do about social science. I think
about composing and how it is defined. I think about training

for artists and where the standards and definitions of a field arise, who they serve, what they preserve, and what they eliminate. I think often about the inevitability of change.

Artists choose to make public expression through exhibitions, performances, written words and the like. They are involved in the communicative process all the time. If you are an artist, that is what you mean to be doing. Otherwise you would never get out of bed. You would dream dances, poems, music, paintings, buildings. Every artist wants a response from his or her own time. This response and exchange is not achieved by plots and games. It is an insult to an audience to assume to know their limits, what they will understand or perceive. The emphasis must be on the work, esthetically, philosophically, socially, with which the artist means to communicate.

Artists are still suspect in our culture and hold a very tenuous place. The products of the artist circulate, for the most part, outside the mainstream of the lives of most people. This is caused by current definitions of art and artists as well as the economics of artistic existence.

The economics of artistic existence and the manner in which art is marketed have a large influence on the decisions that the artist makes, the resulting art produced and the way in which these products and performances are perceived as art or not by the consumer-audience. Mostly artists prefer to ignore this, yet are always bellyaching about it in disguised form. There is still among some a mistaken belief that making the right moves, receiving a status grant, being at the correct social gathering will bring the artist to the attention of the timely gallery owner, publisher or agent and then the doors to success will open. Although some have made it this way, it does not solve the problem by any means and certainly leaves a lot to be desired as a lifestyle. These economic pressures tend to produce a divorce between the artist and the large public. Much art in our time has become increasingly hermetic and the life an artist leads continues to be surrounded by various myths. The familiar ones deal with deprivation and suffering as necessary for artistic activity. Another is that artists, in order to function, must not lead ordinary lives, but engage in esoteric revels with inspiration and the muse. There is not much sense of art as work and, in that way at least, as an ordinary part of life.

This might be the place to talk about the impulse to art, or why, if it is all so awful, people choose to become artists. On that subject I am not able to do more than be descriptive. I do know that no artist can do more than express his or her time more or less perfectly. In fact that is what artists do. An artist organizes material that is available to everyone. There is a necessity to perform this act I'm calling organization. I know for myself the desire to put things together is irrepressible. Where, one might ask, does the imagination enter. Imagination is not mysterious. Permitting yourself to use it fully is not something we are encouraged to do and therein lies the mystery. Philosophy, history, science, the development of worldview, attention to detail and the overview. These are food for the imagination. I don't know why an artist chooses one medium over another. Perhaps it's opportunity.

The power of art lies in its ability and necessity to illuminate the time in which it is made. There are certain formal considerations to all the arts. Time, both in small units such as internal rhythm and phrases and longer ones such as the length of a work or the time factor involved in how a painting or sculpture draws your eyes over its surface. Space, both axial and immediate, also environmental. Structure, or the way in which a work is divided into parts and exists as a whole. Order, or the logic of the arrangement of materials and finally, "tone," or the expressive-emotional factor which is both intended and accidental. In practice these elements are bound together and are only separated for analysis.

In order to develop the uses of formal concepts suitably expressive of our own lives, we must be aware of the events and discoveries which influence our own times. I'm not speaking of a false hipness where tradition and the past are denigrated and only the new and faddish are extolled.

Current technology makes time and order good examples. If I can send a message and have it received as fast as I speak or think it, it is very different than if it takes me a year to deliver it by sail power or on foot. There are ways to condense messages, scramble them and have them instantly available. There are devices which can receive and store tremendous amounts of information and swiftly perform operations with this information which would take men and women many lifetimes to accomplish. Film is another example where, through technology, time and order can be dealt with in a non-linear fashion. We can also through newly developed instruments know about the intimate structures of natural phenomena both organic and inorganic. This knowledge affects art and changes it, gives the imagination new landscapes to range in. The arts that are most readily affected are those where the potential for other than descriptive expression is inherent in the non-verbal character of the medium, such as contemporary dance, music, visual arts. Speech is slow, dance is fast.

These formal elements and the concepts behind their use give art the character it possesses and also place it in historical perspective. The notion of historical perspective saves the individual from wasteful ideas of self-importance and immutable concepts. Ideas do not belong to individuals, but to everyone. No idea is so precious that it should be hoarded. There is always another idea behind the one just given away.

I used to keep very elaborate journals. In my mother's garage there is a dresser, five drawers full of notebooks. Essays and speculations about most of the things I have done as a dancer. These books are elaborate far beyond a workbook or record keeping. They also served as that. Lately my appetite for this kind of journal keeping has diminished. There was in my mind some confusion about permanence, about capturing or keeping so I could savor it at some future date. The problems of having work produced for independent artists are severe. Journal keeping is a poor, but not totally unsatisfying translation. A dance disappears as you see it. A movie of a dance is a dream. A description of a dance is just that. The nature of dance includes impermanence. This is both an opportunity and a problem.

I have tried to make the most of the opportunities that the nature of my field presents. To move away from the middle neutral, that obvious set of moves and appearances which define the field most narrowly. Eight years ago musician-composer Bill Dixon and I began to collaborate in composing and producing works involving both music and dance and in teaching composition to musicians and dancers. We discussed, planned and developed together all the aspects of the work we were composing. We practiced together, criticized each other and held workshops for the musicians and dancers who worked with us. We considered the pieces we composed as being created by both of us and not belonging to one another. Our collaborative position was not readily accepted. We found ourselves involved in much theoretical discussion and demand for explanation about our competence to "invade" each other's field. We thought and planned ways to organize artistic activities to benefit both the artists and the public.

I began at that time to work seriously in improvisation, not as a way of gathering material or making preparations which would then be transformed by other means into a "composition," but improvisation as the sole method of composition. Improvisation as I see it means composing and performing simultaneously. All the forming elements and decisions which exist in the longer method apply here as well. One considers structure, order, space, time, materials and "tone," and one practices daily to make these decisions quickly, consciously and with control. In the last three years I have used this method exclusively.

At the beginning of this period there were many struggles. I had to come to terms with all of my definitions of order and structure. I had to expand my ideas of what dance movement was and could be. What provided me with encouragement and material for study was the example of the improvisational tradition of Black Music, particularly in its most contemporary aspects as demonstrated by Bill Dixon and others.

The methods used in work have implications beyond their immediate artistic use. Improvisation depends very much on the abilities of all the performers involved. They must bring themselves to the task without reservation and they must bring their decision-making power as well.

There are several ways in which decision making and control may be exercised in composition. Picture a scale ranging from total control in the hands of one individual, to a situation of complete collaboration of all the performers involved. After spending most of my career as a dancer-choreographer at one end of the scale I have now moved to the other. This move came out of the needs of work, the benefit to the work and existence in general. I think it is important to say there is no sacrifice of leadership, nor is there any loss of "individuality." Quite the opposite. Aspects of both come forward in a unique fashion from all involved. Experience brings with it knowledge. This does not disappear. Those who are in the earlier stages of their career bring to decisions the knowledge of their time and experiences. One does not negate the other. They fit together very neatly. It is not enough to agree to work collaboratively. It involves constant effort and a continuing critical attention to the processes involved, both artistic and social.

My current position has brought changes, but some ideas remain fixed. I still retain opposition to journalistic criticism and "higher criticism" as it currently affects artists and audience. It seems mostly to serve the persons who write it. In my experience it certainly does not help the artist or inform the public in any serious way about the nature of the work, the ideas involved or in many cases what actually took place. Criticism increasingly has come to mean tearing works and performers apart in a negative and cynical fashion. Too much store, especially by younger artists, is placed on the words of the critics. In the formative part of a career not only is it important to develop skills, to know the history and evolution of the field, but also to achieve a sense of the worth of your own ideas and judgment. In dance, perhaps more than the other arts, the basic unit, the tool is the self. That tool has to be sharpened and tested, permitted to range in an atmosphere which encourages examination and analysis, and is primarily non-judgmental, which focuses on the development of standards rather than having them superimposed as rules which must be first unquestioningly followed and then, only as the grey hairs begin to appear, be discarded. We must create situations which encourage the release of the imagination, which makes study natural and desirable and which brings artists into respectful and encouraging relationships with each other as opposed to the more competitive style of artists of the historical past. It is important to create spaces where artist and audience can each do their communicative work with the greatest interchange, mutual concern and benefit.

THE
MIND IS
A MUSCLE

Yvonne Rainer
1934–

Y vonne Rainer, born in San Francisco, was one of the major
avant-garde choreographers of the sixties and an original
member of the Judson Dance Theater. She studied dance with
Martha Graham, Merce Cunningham, Anna Halprin, and Edith
Stephen and was a composition student with Robert Dunn. Rainer
began to choreograph in 1960. In addition to her company and the
Judson group, she performed with several other choreographers, including James Waring and Judith Dunn.

Rainer's works focus on natural movement and simple tasks. As
one of the young rebels who moved away from rigid dance technique,
Rainer choreographed within the scope of minimalist art. She worked
with artists Robert Morris and Robert Rauschenberg. In 1968,
Rainer began to integrate short films into her live performances and,
by 1975, had made a complete transition to filmmaking. She has
created several feature-length films, shown her work internationally,
and has prints of her films in the archives of major institutions
around the world.

In 1975 she published a retrospective survey of her work entitled
Yvonne Rainer: Work: 1961–73. "The Mind is a Muscle," from
the dance of the same name, was originally written in 1966.

A Quasi Survey of Some "Minimalist" Tendencies in the Quantitatively
Minimal Dance Activity Midst the Plethora, or an Analysis of Trio A

OBJECTS	DANCES
eliminate or minimize	
1. role of artist's hand	1. phrasing
2. hierarchical relationships of parts	2. development and climax
3. texture	3. variation: rhythm, shape, dynamics
4. figure reference	4. character
5. illusionism	5. performance
6. complexity and detail	6. variety: phases and the spatial field
7. monumentality	7. the virtuosic feat and the fully extended body
substitute	
1. factory fabrication	1. energy equality and found movement
2. unitary forms, modules	2. equality of parts, repetition
3. uninterrupted surface	3. repetition or discrete events
4. nonreferential forms	4. neutral performance
5. literalness	5. task or tasklike activity
6. simplicity	6. singular action, event, or tone
7. human scale	7. human scale

Although the benefit to be derived from making a one-to-one relationship between aspects of so-called minimal sculpture and recent dancing is questionable, I have drawn up a chart that does exactly that. Those who needed alternatives to subtle distinction making will be elated, but nevertheless such a device may serve as a shortcut to ploughing through some of the things that have been happening in a specialized area of dancing and once stated can be ignored or culled from at will.

It should not be thought that the two groups of elements are mutually exclusive ("eliminate" and "substitute"). Much work being done today—both in theater and art—has concerns in both categories. Neither should it be thought that the type of dance I shall discuss has been influenced exclusively by art. The changes in theater and dance reflect changes in ideas about man and his environment that have affected all the arts. That dance should reflect these changes at all is of interest, since for obvious reasons it has always been the most isolated and inbred of the arts. What is perhaps unprecedented in the short history of the modern dance is the close correspondence between concurrent developments in dance and the plastic arts.

Isadora Duncan went back to the Greeks; Humphrey and Graham* used primitive ritual and/or music for structuring, and although the people who came out of the Humphrey-Graham companies and were active during the thirties and forties shared socio-political concerns and activity in common with artists of the period, their work did not reflect any direct influence from or dialogue with the art so much as a reaction to the time. (Those who took off in their own directions in the forties and fifties—Cunningham, Shearer, Litz, Marsicano et al. —must be appraised individually. Such a task is beyond the scope of this article.) The one previous area of correspondence might be German Expressionism and Mary Wigman and her followers, but photographs and descriptions of the work show little connection.

Within the realm of movement invention—and I am talking for the time being about movement generated by means other than accomplishment of a task or dealing with an object—the most impressive change has been in the attitude to phrasing, which can be defined as the way in which energy is distributed in the execution of a movement or series of movements. What makes one kind of movement different from another is not so much variations in arrangements of parts of the body as differences in energy investment.

It is important to distinguish between real energy and what I shall call "apparent" energy. The former refers to actual output in terms of physical expenditure on the part of the performer. It is common to hear a dance teacher tell a student that he is using "too much energy" or that a particular movement does not require "so much energy." This view of energy is related to a notion of economy and ideal movement technique. Unless otherwise indicated, what I shall be talking about here is "apparent" energy, or what is seen in terms of motion and stillness rather than of actual work, regardless of the physiolog-

---

*In the case of Graham, it is hardly possible to relate her work to anything outside of theatre, since it was usually dramatic and psychological necessity that determined it.

ical or kinesthetic experience of the dancer. The two observations—that of the performer and that of the spectator—do not always correspond. A vivid illustration of this is my *Trio A:* upon completion two of us are always dripping with sweat while the third is dry. The correct conclusion to draw is not that the dry one is expending less energy, but that the dry one is a "non-sweater."

Much of the western dancing we are familiar with can be characterized by a particular distribution of energy: maximal output or "attack" at the beginning of a phrase,* recovery at the end, with energy often arrested somewhere in the middle. This means that one part of the phrase—usually the part that is the most still—becomes the focus of attention, registering like a photograph or suspended moment of climax. In the Graham-oriented modern dance these climaxes can come one on the heels of the other. In types of dancing that depend on less impulsive controls, the climaxes are farther apart and are not so dramatically "framed." Where extremes in tempi are imposed, this ebb-and-flow of effort is also pronounced: in the instance of speed the contrast between movement and rest is sharp, and in the adagio, or supposedly continuous kind of phrasing, the execution of transitions demonstrates more subtly the mechanics of getting from one point of still "registration" to another.

The term "phrase" can also serve as a metaphor for a longer or total duration containing beginning, middle, and end. Whatever the implications of a continuity that contains high points or focal climaxes, such an approach now seems to be excessively dramatic and more simply, unnecessary.

Energy has been used to implement heroic more-than-human technical feats and to maintain a more-than-human look of physical extension, which is familiar as the dancer's muscular "set." In the early days of the Judson Dance Theatre someone wrote an article and asked, "Why are they so intent on just being themselves?" It is not accurate to say that every-

*The term "phrase" must he distinguished from "phrasing." A phrase is simply two or more consecutive movements, while phrasing, as noted previously, refers to the manner of execution.

one at that time had this in mind. (I certainly didn't; I was more involved in experiencing a lion's share of ecstasy and madness than in "being myself" or doing a job.) But where the question applies, it might be answered on two levels: 1) The artifice of performance has been reevaluated in that action, or what one does, is more interesting and important than the exhibition of character and attitude, and that action can best be focused on through the submerging of the personality; so ideally one is not even oneself, one is a neutral "doer." 2) The display of technical virtuosity and the display of the dancer's specialized body no longer make any sense. Dancers have been driven to search for an alternative context that allows for a more matter-of-fact, more concrete, more banal quality of physical being in performance, a context wherein people are engaged in actions and movements making a less spectacular demand on the body and in which skill is hard to locate.

It is easy to see why the *grand jeté* (along with its ilk) had to be abandoned. One cannot "do" a *grand jeté;* one must "dance" it to get it done at all, i.e., invest it with all the necessary nuances of energy distribution that will produce the look of climax together with a still, suspended extension in the middle of the movement. Like a romantic, overblown plot this particular kind of display—with its emphasis on nuance and skilled accomplishment, its accessibility to comparison and interpretation, its involvement with connoisseurship, its introversion, narcissism, and self-congratulatoriness—has finally in this decade exhausted itself, closed back on itself, and perpetuates itself solely by consuming its own tail.

The alternatives that were explored now are obvious: stand, walk, run, eat, carry bricks, show movies, or move or be moved by some thing rather than oneself. Some of the early activity in the area of self-movement utilized games, "found" movement (walking, running, etc.), and people with no previous training. (One of the most notable of these early efforts was Steve Paxton's solo, *Transit,* in which he performed movement by "marking" it. "Marking" is what dancers do in rehearsal when they do not want to expend the full amount of energy required for the execution of a given movement. It has a very special

look, tending to blur boundaries between consecutive movements.) These descriptions are not complete. Different people
have sought different solutions.

Since I am primarily a dancer, I am interested in finding
solutions primarily in the area of moving oneself, however
many excursions I have made into pure and not-so-pure thing-
moving. In 1964 I began to play around with simple one- and
two-motion phrases that required no skill and little energy and
contained few accents. The way in which they were put
together was indeterminate, or decided upon in the act of performing, because at that time the idea of a different kind of
continuity as embodied in transitions or connections between
phrases did not seem to be as important as the material itself.
The result was that the movements or phrases appeared as isolated bits framed by stoppages. Underscored by their smallness
and separateness, they projected as perverse *tours de force*. Every
time "elbow-wiggle" came up one felt like applauding. It was
obvious that the idea of an unmodulated energy output as
demonstrated in the movement was not being applied to the
continuity. A continuum of energy was required. Duration and
transition had to be considered.

Which brings me to *The Mind is a Muscle, Trio A*. Without
giving an account of the drawn-out process through which this
four-and-a-half-minute movement series (performed simultaneously by three people) was made, let me talk about its implications in the direction of movement-as-task or movement-as-
object.

One of the most singular elements in it is that there are no
pauses between phrases. The phrases themselves often consist of
separate parts, such as consecutive limb articulations—"right leg,
left leg, arms, jump," etc.—but the end of each phrase merges
immediately into the beginning of the next with no observable
accent. The limbs are never in a fixed, still relationship and they
are stretched to their fullest extension only in transit, creating
the impression that the body is constantly engaged in transitions.

Another factor contributing to the smoothness of the continuity is that no one part of the series is made any more important than any other. For four and a half minutes a great vari-

ety of movement shapes occur, but they are of equal weight and are equally emphasized. This is probably attributable both to the sameness of physical "tone" that colors all the movements and to the attention to the pacing. I can't talk about one without talking about the other.

The execution of each movement conveys a sense of unhurried control. The body is weighty without being completely relaxed. What is seen is a control that seems geared to the *actual* time it takes the *actual* weight of the body to go through the prescribed motions, rather than an adherence to an imposed ordering of time. In other words, the demands made on the body's (actual) energy resources appear to be commensurate with the task—be it getting up from the floor, raising an arm, tilting the pelvis, etc.—much as one would get out of a chair, reach for a high shelf, or walk down stairs when one is not in a hurry.* The movements are not mimetic, so they do not remind one of such actions, but I like to think that in their manner of execution they have the factual quality of such actions.

Of course, I have been talking about the "look" of the movements. In order to achieve this look in a continuity of separate phrases that does not allow for pauses, accents, or stillness, one must bring to bear many different degrees of effort just in getting from one thing to another. Endurance comes into play very much with its necessity for conserving (actual) energy (like the long-distance runner). The irony here is in the reversal of a kind of illusionism: I have exposed a type of effort where it has been traditionally concealed and have concealed phrasing where it has been traditionally displayed.

So much for phrasing. My *Trio A* contained other elements mentioned in the chart that have been touched on in passing, not being central to my concerns of the moment. For example, the "problem" of performance was dealt with by never permitting the performers to confront the audience. Either the gaze was averted or the head was engaged in movement. The desired

---

*I do not mean to imply that the demand of musical or metric phrasing makes dancing look effortless. What it produces is a different kind of effort, where the body looks more extended, "pulled up," highly energized, ready to go, etc. The dancer's "set" again.

effect was a worklike rather than exhibitionlike presentation.

I shall deal briefly with the remaining categories on the chart as they relate to *Trio A*. Variation was not a method of development. No one of the individual movements in the series was made by varying a quality of any other one. Each is intact and separate with respect to its nature. In a strict sense neither is there any repetition (with the exception of occasional consecutive traveling steps). The series progresses by the fact of one discrete thing following another. This procedure was consciously pursued as a change from my previous work, which often had one identical thing following another—either consecutively or recurrently. Naturally the question arises as to what constitutes repetition. In *Trio A,* where there is no consistent consecutive repetition, can the simultaneity of three identical sequences be called repetition? Or can the consistency of energy tone be called repetition? Or does repetition apply only to successive specific actions?

All of these considerations have supplanted the desire for dance structures wherein elements are connected thematically (through variation) and for a diversity in the use of phrases and space. I think two assumptions are implicit here: 1) A movement is a complete and self-contained event; elaboration in the sense of varying some aspect of it can only blur its distinctness; and 2) Dance is hard to see. It must either be made less fancy, or the fact of that intrinsic difficulty must be emphasized to the point that it becomes almost impossible to see.

Repetition can serve to enforce the discreteness of a movement, objectify it, make it more objectlike. It also offers an alternative way of ordering material, literally making the material easier to see. That most theatre audiences are irritated by it is not yet a disqualification.

My *Trio A* dealt with the "seeing" difficulty by dint of its continual and unremitting revelation of gestural detail that did *not* repeat itself, thereby focusing on the fact that the material could not easily be encompassed.

There is at least one circumstance that the chart does not include (because it does not relate to "minimization"), viz., the static singular object versus the object with interchangeable parts. The dance equivalent is the indeterminate performance that produces variations ranging from small details to a total image. Usually indeterminacy has been used to change the sequentialness—either phrases or larger sections—of a work, or to permute the details of a work. It has also been used with respect to timing. Where the duration of separate, simultaneous events is not prescribed exactly, variations in the relationship of these events occur. Such is the case with the trio I have been speaking about, in which small discrepancies in the tempo of individually executed phrases result in the three simultaneous performances constantly moving in and out of phase and in and out of synchronization. The overall look of it is constant from one performance to another, but the distribution of bodies in space at any given instant changes.

I am almost done. *Trio A* is the first section of *The Mind is a Muscle*. There are six people involved and four more sections. *Trio B* might be described as a VARIATION of *Trio A* in its use of unison with three people; they move in exact unison throughout. *Trio A* is about the EFFORTS of two men and a woman in getting each other aloft in VARIOUS ways while REPEATING the same diagonal SPACE pattern throughout. In *Horses* the group travels about as a unit, recurrently REPEATING six different ACTIONS. *Lecture* is a solo that REPEATS the MOVEMENT series of *Trio A*. There will be at least three more sections.*

There are many concerns in this dance. The concerns may appear to fall on my tidy chart as randomly dropped toothpicks might. However, I think there is sufficient separating-out in my work as well as that of certain of my contemporaries to justify an attempt at organizing those points of departure from previous work. Comparing the dance to Minimal Art provided a convenient method of organization. Omissions and overstatements are a hazard of any systematizing in art. I hope that some degree of redress will be offered by whatever clarification results from this essay.

---

*This article was written before the final version of *The Mind is a Muscle* had been made. (*Mat, Stairs,* and *Film* are not discussed.)

TALKING WITH
PILOBOLUS

An Interview by Elvi Moore

*P*ilobolus was born in the winter of the academic year 1970-
1971 on the Dartmouth College campus. Four students in a
modern dance class, with no previous dance experience, produced a unique, organic, eleven-minute dance, and named it Pilobolus
for a fungus.

Pilobolus Dance Theatre was founded in 1971 by Moses Pendleton
and Jonathan Wolken. They were joined later that year by Robby
Barnett, by Martha Clarke and their original teacher Alison Chase in
1973, and by Michael Tracy in 1974. Now with four of the original
directors and six additional dancers, the group continues to attract ac-
claim and prizes with their innovative, athletic approach to dance.

Pilobolus originally substituted athleticism for traditional dance
technique. They have since blended the two, as they continue to develop. The cooperative creative effect achieved by support of one another's
weight in unusual ways allows the dancers to explore new possibilities
of movement, new ways of performing old movement, and altogether
new images. The result is an entirely new aesthetics, and an often sculptural effect. The excitement is in the dancer's daring and in their elim-
ination of effort from the difficult and sometimes seemingly dangerous
dances.

"Pilobolus has twelve legs but one soul." The trust and the unity is
reflected in the following interview with Pilobolus, made in 1976.

Elvi Moore. It sounds as though you constantly hear yourselves
described as a gymnastic/acrobatic team, is that correct?

Martha Clarke. Yes, but none of us has any background in acrobatics or gymnastics.

Alison Chase. I think people use it because they don't know how to define us and it is an easy way of description. We don't use traditional dance vocabulary and so they think that it's mainly gymnastic vocabulary.

Moses Pendleton. We do use gymnastics and acrobatics, but it is also true that we draw from all kinds of movement, whether labeled modern dance or whatever. We don't have anything against being upside down or off vertically. People see that only as being gymnastic, but for us, it is a vehicle to show a particular image or something choreographically we feel works in the piece. I think the thing that bothers us is the fact that "gymnastic" usually means stunts and feats that are done simply for effect. We don't feel that we're just out there doing or showing tricks. There is something else, at least a concept, an idea, behind those particular movements.

Robby Barnett. Moreover, I think our new work is moving away from the earlier vocabulary that we have been more involved in up to now. Our last two pieces are not even gymnastic, and there is not much dancing in them.

Elvi. There certainly is evident an evolution, it seems to me, from the original pieces to Monkshood Farewell and the untitled piece. You are going into something completely different now, into more thematic works, is that correct?

Martha. Yes, with a more theatrical impulse. I think we now use the linked movement in the earlier techniques merely as a means to realize the images and maybe the theatrical ideas that we have. Whereas, before that, technique was an end in itself.

Moses. In the earlier pieces, like *Ciona,* we were more concerned simply with the movement, the shape, the designs and the musicality of the piece. This new untitled work, more than any of the previous pieces, is beginning to deal with the relationships between people and is much more a theater piece.

Elvi. Martha said that none of you have had acrobatic or gymnastic training. How did your whole style evolve? I know that the two ladies are dance trained, and were the rest of you trained by Alison?

Alison. Oh, I don't take any credit for their talent.

Robby. I think to a degree the reason it went the way it did was that there's a certain sort of release, almost athletic energy, and when we moved, it wasn't with a trained dancer's body. Because of our athletic background, instead of doing extensions and doing turns on center, we started by holding on to each other. We were interested in the design; it was something that we could control very easily without training.

Alison. The first dance of Pilobolus was the defining piece. I had never seen people use their bodies to create shapes in tension like that. I'd say that this was the piece that defined their early style.

Moses. When we first began, there was Jonathan, myself, and another fellow, Steve Johnson. The original piece that we did was titled *Pilobolus*. I felt very paranoid about just getting up and doing a dance. We felt that maybe we couldn't dance, so why try to? When we began, we didn't really feel free, moving in space individually. We literally *had* to hang onto each other. We all figured that we could at least do that much, and it was something larger than any one body could make. It wasn't so difficult if you did create this shape, a thing that moved. We began to play around by combining bodies.

Elvi. How do you go about keeping your bodies in shape; in a systematic training or all different ways?

Alison. We do nothing collectively in terms of training. Everybody does what they need to do for their own body. Some of the guys have started to do ballet barre and Martha and I try to help them with that.

Moses. The women now are jogging and lifting weights and working out in the gym and we're going to ballet classes!

Jonathan Wolken. We constantly wrestle on mats.

Moses. Alison runs four miles a day. I used to run all the time—now I never lift a foot or never break into stride.

Elvi. Why are you getting into ballet exercises now?

Jonathan. That's an individual thing. For example, *this* person [pointing to himself] is not getting into ballet classes yet. It's a totally open kind of thing in the company.

Martha. I think it helps to push the technical possibilities and to refine them.

Moses. In order to even develop or change the choreography sometimes you can work by thinking of a new dance. Another way to go about it is to simply train your body differently so that you can do new movements that offer a different vocabulary to make a new dance. If we worked to do things we weren't able to do before, then the next piece might involve a different vocabulary, therefore a different choreography.

Jonathan. The point I'm trying to make, probably in a backward way, is that despite the fact that one's movement possibilities are increased, the choreography seems to take a direction of its own. If we use training of any kind, it's more toward choreographic ends than for training itself.

Moses. We're also finding that the training for a particular piece, *Ciona,* for example, would be much more effective if people could stand on their own two feet a little better, could move more easily through space.

Martha. The more technical facility you have, the more you're able to explore. That's why I feel we should all be getting stronger and refining what we have. I think the company is dancing better each season. It's from doing work. It's from performing it all. Jonathan, you're the only one in the company who is not in favor of this, and that's your prerogative, but I think that the other people who are doing the barre would feel that they're improving.

Jonathan. Well, I feel that I'm improving without a barre. That's not to say I don't feel I'm improving. For that matter, I can't say that people would not normally improve anyway if they would just pay attention to their movements. It's not the barre, it's not the wall, it's not the set-up, it's the idea of concentrating on the movement.

Moses. It's not just the barre. I think the point is that you pay attention to your needs and you work on your body.

Elvi. You all feel, though, that some discipline in training your own bodies in your own way is very good in keeping sharp.

Jonathan. Without a doubt, even when we approach the barre in a different way. Martha might do a very traditional barre, sixteen of these, sixteen of those. Alison might do something of a traditional barre too. Whereas, if I went to the barre, and when I've seen the other men in the company go to the barre, I wouldn't use it in the same way. I might pull or tug against completely different things.

Alison. I think, given that the women are trained and the men are untrained, there might be an area between that we could explore if they had the training that approximated ours or tried to meet ours. I think that Martha and I have met the boys' way of moving. I think it would be nice if they could meet our way of moving at some point in time.

Moses. I think the point is that whether you do a barre, or stretch, or just hang upside down, the difference is the attention that you try to give your body to make it work better each day. Somehow that will reflect itself in the choreography.

Elvi. What about choreography, the creative endeavors in choreography, can you talk about that a little bit? How do you start a new work? Does it always begin with a definite movement idea?

Jonathan. Before we start talking about this, we should probably add a word of precaution that everyone in this company has distinct and probably radically different ideas about what is done, how it's done, and how it begins, so that people will speak differently for themselves when they answer this.

Martha. I would say that with the new piece, we started with the notion of a man under a woman's skirt and the idea of being tall and small, of being able to just feel the movement possibilities within that structure of having somebody under your skirt.

Alison. And the image possibility. There's that element of fantasy of being street level and being twice that high, and then this form, that shape have various other image suggestions.

Martha. The psychological line that the dance takes means we find movements all of a sudden. We don't say we want to make this apparent or that apparent; it's constructed rather blindly in a way, and then all of a sudden certain things will be revealed to both. This is what the relationship is about, but it happens after the movement has been invented and sewn together.

Moses. To continue what Martha was saying, when we first begin a piece, we might have a vague idea of what we want to do. We may spend a couple of weeks on what we call gathering material; in a way it's like an improvisation. We go into a studio and just work and play on various moves. Eventually one move may link to another or you may find a particular image that will allow you to start thinking in terms of where a piece may go, or it might develop. In the process of those three weeks you might find three or four sets—bits of material for different pieces. Eventually we begin to focus in on one particular idea from the movement, from the images that emerge from the movement. Then the piece begins to develop. After a couple of weeks the ideas become formed, and you begin to work more seriously on movement that has something to do with that original idea which came out of a certain type of improvisation.

Martha. Then there might also be phrases that don't seem to have any home. The dance might go fine A to F, then suddenly you've got M-N-O, and you have to then think of an idea that would make a legitimate connection theatrically.

Moses. Further on, the ideas become more manifest, and you almost start making movements out of the ideas. Whereas, as Martha says, to fill in particular gaps, you start thinking of certain types of movement to complete a concept.

Alison. With this new piece, there is a lot of material that we just haven't developed yet. We have a whole bar scene, a saloon scene, and we become dwarves with these skirts that are very long. Martha and I are transformed into dwarves by putting our knees up into our tops, while the guys would still be inside the skirt, but there's no torso and they move out gradually, but we have not used it yet.

Robby. It can be very frustrating, to have material that's marvelous, but it just doesn't fit. As Alison said, we have a whole range of terrifically comedic movements using these big women as tops and street ladies, a lot of very funny slapstick stuff that we don't feel is appropriate the way the piece is going.

Elvi. Are you satisfied with the new piece as it is now?

Jonathan. We're in the process of beginning to mount a lot of free choreography into our things. As soon as we get the

time to go at it again, we'll change it because there are problems in this piece, especially because of the score, which is for
us much more liquid. It has been composed for an orchestra,
it's been recorded by an orchestra. If it's going to be amended,
it has to be assembled. It can be done for sure, but it's a much
more difficult process and one has to look at editing in a different way.

Robby. I think we'll attempt to make our piece fit the score
at this point. It's perfectly possible for them to make room
beyond what the score holds. We will have to extend the score,
but I think certainly we're going to try to fit whatever changes
we do inside that.

Moses. We worked on it furiously, and even unfinished, it was
very helpful to gain a perspective on it by performing it. Even
in the rough stage, because it gives us a chance to get away from
it and look at it and have a certain response to it. It allows us
to see the piece a bit more objectively.

Elvi. Where do you foresee yourselves going now, more into
the theatrical works like the new untitled one?

Robby. I think for the next year, as we hone this piece and
change it, we are going to be involved in smaller works that
will give us each a chance to explore the things that we happen to be particularly interested in. I think it's hard to tell what
[the] company will turn out next. It's hard to say what out
direction will be. For example, when the original four decided
to ask the women to join. At the time, we thought we'd just try
it out and see how it went, thinking at least it would keep
things moving forward, rather than sort of stymying us all. So
they came along with us, and after a certain period of time we
all sort of melted together.

Martha. In the beginning, Allison and I were not well integrated in the group. It took a year and a half, nearly two years,
to make it work where everyone was on kind of equal footing.

Moses. One of the difficulties was that they had their pieces
that they were doing and we had ours. Obviously, it doesn't
look like an integrated company if the women want to do their
business and the men come on and want to do theirs. Then we
began to try to fit the women into a man's vocabulary, which

they have done wonderfully. It's unbelievable. Alison would come in and simply do a male role in obviously a very strong man-type dance. Both of them have done that very well and now we're beginning to evolve, like this new piece, which is very much a woman's theme. It's about women, and Robby and I, for instance, are trying to think in terms of women's psychology, which is different from the women trying to do men's movement.

Elvi. I think the integration is quite clear. In your first appearance at the University of Chicago a year and a half ago, and again in January, I felt a tremendous difference in the way the company now handles its work.

Moses. Monkshood was the first piece that we, as a company of four men and two women, began to choreograph from the start. Obviously, when you make a piece, if you begin the choreography with the people who are going to be in the piece, everything is integrated because it's wedded at the start.

Martha. Also, we had a year under our belts. We knew about each other's sense of humor, the kind of twist that we wanted to take.

Elvi. How do you handle requests from other dancers to join your company?

Jonathan. Bringing people into the company, this is an interesting subject. We think about it a lot, talk about it some too. Our company, because it's different, because of the fact that there is no central thing, and because we work cooperatively, the idea of bringing an outside influence into the company is not just a lark. It's a temporary release, as we've mentioned before—you know, it gives us all a kind of release of tension. But the long-run effect is really a serious consideration of how we'll get along as an expanded family. The interaction of the company is very intense, and complete.

Martha. Also, we've achieved a group aesthetic. We all have different ideas about the dances, but when something good happens, we all know it's good. The minute you bring a new element in on a more or less permanent basis, it risks this.

Robby. We're also somewhat resistant to people who are almost too full of energy and too full of ideas because there is a certain personal subjugation that goes into being a corporate entity.

Jonathan. If all of us spoke all of our ideas all of the time, the confusion would be totally out of hand. So we have a collective filter, and it's really a pretty involved process.

Elvi. Part of the whole difference appears to be that, not only are you talking about making dances, but you're also talking about a whole lifestyle which certainly makes Pilobolus very unique, and would make someone coming in go through a difficult adjustment period.

Moses. We try to function on a type of self-discipline and sort of democratic situation and at times, I suppose, try to take advantage of it.

Jonathan. It's idealistically an approach. Just the fact that we manage to eke out an existence and keep centered without falling apart is a remarkable feat.

Moses. You wonder sometimes why people get themselves into group situations in the first place; maybe because they find energy and ideas from it, and the fact that they can't really feel that they function well by themselves. It certainly happens in many groups as the group matures and establishes itself. People, after a while, growing older, begin to have their own sensibility and need for individuality, and I think *that* is even happening in our company. There comes a point where you wonder whether the group is actually feeding the individual, which it must do always. I don't think a group works simply because you're doing it totally for the group; you're doing it for yourself also. That's the thing that becomes more and more difficult in this company as people begin to have a certain sense of their own aesthetic sensibility. To constantly compromise in a group in which individuals are trying very hard to develop as individuals: that's the tension we're always working on.

Martha. I hope that what we'll achieve is an objectivity about the work itself, with the individual adding to the work and gaining from the work in order to expand the individual's career. Each person has to grow within the framework, everybody has to be given the chance to grow.

Moses. At times, for some people in the group it becomes threatening because they feel that they see another individual in the group taking off. That for me is not too much of a threat to Pilobolus, but a necessary course for it to take. Although it may not be the most efficient way to keep this company together, it has to allow itself to become inefficient, allow itself to accommodate, to listen to personal needs as best it can.

Jonathan. The only thing that can be said in all truth is that the relationship between the individual and the company is constantly fluctuating and changing and re-establishing new balances. Sometimes the thing is out of control, sometimes it's totally in control. Individuals are always related to Pilobolus, this third entity, in fluctuating ways. So it's really quite a boiling pot. You never can say exactly where it is or exactly where it's going or where it might go.

Elvi. I think that's really an amazing feat, four and a half years with only one change in personnel. Let me wish you continued success as you continue to grow as individuals and as a group. Many of us will certainly be watching and hoping to enjoy your expanding talents for a long time to come.

DIALOGUE ON DANCE

Trisha Brown
1936–

Douglas Dunn
1942–

*B*orn *in Aberdeen, Washington, Trisha Brown studied with Anna Halprin while a dance major at Mills College. She went to New York in 1960, and in 1962 became a founding member of the Judson Dance Theater. She formed her own company in 1970, the same year that she became a founding member of the improvisational dance theater company Grand Union.*

Brown creates work in cycles, typically exploring movement ideas over the course of three pieces. Her early work often exploited the urban architecture, and was presented in such settings as roof-tops, rafts on a lake, or on the sides of buildings. She has worked with mathematical and geometrical structures and collaborated with artists such as Robert Rauschenberg and Laurie Anderson to transform traditional stage space. In 1994, Brown performed an entire solo without once facing forwards (If You Couldn't See Me), *and has even embraced Bach's* Musical Offering, *remaining true to form by developing an intricate structure of her own.*

Douglas Dunn grew up in the hills in back of Palo Alto, California. With a background in athletics and ballet, he went to New York to dance in 1968. He performed with Yvonne Rainer and Group from 1968 to 1970, and with Merce Cunningham and Dance Company from 1969 to 1973.

Dunn was also a founding member of the Grand Union and per-

formed with it from 1970 to 1975. In 1971 he began presenting his own work, formed Douglas Dunn & Dancers in 1977, and appeared at the Autumn Festival in Paris in 1978. Dunn has been making dances and performing with his troup at home and abroad ever since.

This conversation conducted for Performing Arts Journal, *is another indication of the cooperative spirit found among the members of the avant-garde of the sixties and seventies.*

Dunn. For *Lazy Madge* I'm working with nine dancers, one at a time, spending about eight to ten hours making about five to ten minutes of material on each person. And I am making duets for myself with several of the people. This seems to come only after I've made solo material for the person. I'm also thinking about making trios using them without me. The dancers I'm working with are people who've studied dance—and they're dancers who're all very different, have different techniques, and strikingly different personalities which becomes very obvious when they're on the space together. I made a solo on each of two women who'd never met. They did their two solos on the space at the same time. They had a strong reaction to one another and the result was very exciting on a dog-meets-dog level as well as on a dance level. I'm trying to not think about all the things I used to think about—that's been my main instruction to myself for this work. Not to pay attention to most of the formal things. So I end up paying attention to simply what I have to tell a person to do and go through movement that they can remember and keep. So far there is a very strong formality to my work and it's coming out different than if I had paid attention to it.

Brown. What do you mean by formality?

Dunn. Everything. The time, the space, the rhythm, the movement . . . plus any general shape of the piece. I never lay out floor patterns. I try not to have any ideas before I start working with a person. I focus on that person and not just phys-ically; I try to generate imagery off paying attention to them.

Brown. So you make a solo on them.

Dunn. Very specifically. I don't work at all until the people come in. There is also some amount of material which I con-

sider stylistic because it repeats. I just found myself using certain movements more than others.

Brown. How do you do that?

Dunn. For example, the first person I worked with is a short, squarish woman and for some reason when I thought of her certain images came to mind. The second position, for one. I'm allowing imagery to come back into my work. The other formal thing that's going on in the work is that there are very, very short phrases which are almost always stopped. Each phrase is a little rhythmic invention which eventually stops. Then something else begins.

Brown. Is that because you were making the piece in that size segment and stopping and teaching it to them?

Dunn. Not really. It's about having to undercut all the representational imagery that's coming in. Physical imagery—dance movement imagery as well as mime imagery. At this point I don't think of myself as someone with a personal dance style. That's irrelevant to me. What I'm dealing with is what I know about the outside world. So this piece is about that. . . . I'm still relatively dedicated to being functional about getting in and out of things unless there's a specific imagistic reason not to do so. The things that I do which are specifically awkward are made to be awkward. I don't really say I want to make an image of something. I start to make steps, then think of the imagistic possibilities. So it's not as if the imagery comes first. The feeling in the image area develops later. This is new to me.

Brown. I call what you're talking about a position.

Dunn. I'm just making a difference in the degree of attention to images in my work.

Brown. I was wondering if you're allowing that a movement has more meaning than just pure physical imagery.

Dunn. A lot more. But I'm not asking people to perform in a way that they add to that at all. In fact, I'm making difficult movements, so that the dancers struggle with them. That's also one of the things I'm working with.

Brown. What happens if they can't achieve it?

Dunn. Everybody can try to do something of what it is.

Brown. What do you settle for?

Dunn. I haven't yet taken anything away from anybody because they can't do it. Watching them try to do it interests me a lot. I also see the experience of people who have that attitude for learning how to do something. That experience amazes me more and more because it's faded somewhat in me. Having this appetite to learn how to do things they can't do at first helps. They do it.

Whether they do it or not is irrelevant because there is a line of something going on that makes it feel necessary to do the next thing. Sometimes it requires something very awkward. By awkward I mean something difficult, physically or otherwise. People have an appetite for trying to do it, and as long as they have that energy, I'm going to be there. All it accepts is that people come and go. I haven't set up a schedule with nine people and said this is what we're working on and so on. This is going to be some kind of on-going situation until we know whether to keep going.

Brown. But do you intend to have them performing all together at one time in one place?

Dunn. Yeah. And I tend to leave a lot of decisions undecided. I've been making these duets and I haven't been setting at all what I do. It's really that forgetting, not knowing I guess, that is new to me. I've never been in such a dance situation. This approach is for *Lazy Madge:* this is not my approach.

Brown. Right now I'm just at the beginning stage of making a new piece. [*Structured Pieces V* was performed in France at the Fêtes Musicales de la Sainte-Baume in August, 1976.] I don't know how much of what I say will be in the piece. But I've made a section of material which is something like functional movement. Not functional movement, but a logical progression where one movement follows another. Movement B is an obvious movement after A, C is obvious after B. No big jumps. I try not to leave anything out. There are little flashes of eccentricity along the way. This movement goes backward as well as forward. I now have two people who are doing it.

There are points in the phrase (like standing up, sitting, etc.) that are like possible intersections for other obvious moves to go in other directions. I intend to make alternate phrases branching off this main phrase. They will all back up and go forward and possibly even to the right and the left. At this point two people go forward and backward in a three-minute phrase. They start out and go forward. I verbally stop them, back them up, bring them forward, put them in sync with each other. . . . I try to get interesting combinations of the phrase, visually and rhythmically, by verbally manipulating them.

At this point I'd like to put this movement, and a greatly extended phrase of 20 minutes, on to at least four people and try to direct them from outside during the performance. I don't think I'll be dancing in this piece. I've been sitting more and watching my dancers work in front of me, but then I get up to do things and it's hard for me to stay warm. I was thinking about some sort of platform that could be built for me so I could stretch while I'm watching them. When they need me I could get right up. Then I thought I should put pillows on this platform. Then I saw myself sinking down into the pillows, sending messages like paper airplanes out to the dancers.

Dunn. It's very interesting that you should direct the new piece. When I got out of the Merce Cunningham Company and started watching pieces, one of the things I disliked was the frequent modern dance theme of the choreographer as . . . choreographer. I thought I was certainly not going to get involved in *that!* And I'm very involved in it. *Lazy Madge* is about that. It shocks me to death.

Brown. Is the dancing more virtuosic?

Dunn. No. It's much easier to do physically.

Brown. Are you thinking of a dramatic character?

Dunn. No. Not that strong. . . . I don't want to use movement manipulations as a source of invention. I'm involved in retrograde work. . . . I'm thinking of movement in an imagistic way—images that interrupt the line of movement.

Brown. I start with a structure and make movement to fit my concept. . . . I used to always improvise, to have some sort of improvisation in my work—which was purely dealing with my personal resources on the fly in front of the audience. When I began dancing with the Grand Union, I didn't have to do that any more. There was a marked transition in my own work from improvisation, large constructions, and language to movement.

So when I got back into making movement, I used a simple form which was to make 1 movement, repeat it several times and add 2, repeat 1 and 2 several times and add 3, then 4, etc. Movements were wedged in between earlier additions which upset the linear scheme and caused the dance to fatten rather than lengthen—and often in a lopsided manner. I was learning about the form by doing it. It was a messy construction job but I would never go back and correct it. *Primary Accumulation* was only one movement at a time—one, one-two, one-two-three, etc. A pared down and less emotive version, although viewers were emotionally stirred.

Dunn. I think your answer indicates something general which is that there is an interest in dance as an area to experiment with movement problems or performance problems as possibilities—as opposed to a vehicle for expressing what you think about the world. It's like talking—through your dancing—about the kinds of things that interest you about movement, how you put a dance together. What is it about? Your titles suggest that you look at dance as a formal structure. *Accumulation* as a title as opposed to your *Pamplona Stones* points to the structural basis of the piece.

Brown. *Pamplona Stones* was put together through free association which was a break from the more austere *Accumulation* pieces I had been doing. I scripted it before teaching it to the other dancers. It is an imaginary dialogue based on some drawings I had made. It turned out that there was a constant inner dramatic thread in the piece. It was referring back to itself through words and questioning and actions. It got its name through sounds. We were using stones as material very early in the piece and Pamplona rhymed with stones—somewhat. One performer was Spanish and Pamplona is a Spanish town I remembered.

Dunn. The question of what to call one's work is a problem. I think everybody looks around the environment, sees how terms are being used and tries to represent their work as clearly as possible. This was a problem with the Grand Union. We wanted to think of ourselves as doing everything, and just wanted to know how to say that. We didn't call ourselves "dancers" because that was too limited. We chose not to use words like "theatre" or "drama" because we didn't like the association with other theatre. We definitely wanted to be connected with an art position. We used to say "Grand Union is a collaboration of individual artists." People choose the words "dance" or "theatre" according to the elements in their work.

Brown. In the sixties, a trained dancer was a person with a puffed-out ribcage who was designed to project across the footlights in a proscenium arch stage. He or she couldn't necessarily do a natural kind of movement, even a simple one. So what I looked for was a person with a natural, well-coordinated, instinctive ability to move. At that time the whole dance vocabulary was open. It was no longer selected movement or chosen gestures for telling a story within the formal vocabulary of ballet movement. All movement became available for choreographing. . . . *Walking on the Wall* gave the illusion that the audience was overhead, looking down on the tops of the heads of the performers walking and standing below. It also showed what it was, the performance of a simple activity against the principles of gravity. The rigging and technical business of getting up there was in clear view.

Dunn. It was stylized movement in extraordinary circumstances, or ordinary movement in extraordinary circumstances.

Brown. That was developing a skill for an occasion—appearing to be natural in a completely un-natural situation. The "happenings" people used non-actors to do performances and that came before Judson. Also there is a certain look or personality of trained dancers of traditional schools. They train for alikeness, a certain conformity. It was interesting to have people of different personalities and posture and looks about them on the stage. I've been working with combinations of other kinds of movement than natural movement. I've been working with unnatural movement.

Dunn. If we talk historically, what wasn't present as available material for dances in the sixties and which later became available material was stylization. Before the sixties there was no consciousness of certain things as being dance.

Brown. I think the "Twist" helped a lot in the sixties.

Dunn. Rock dancing was a bridge between your daily life, which was still unconscious perhaps, and part of your classroom dance life which was not making available that possibility. . . . When I came to New York in 1968 and Yvonne Rainer was looking for people fresh off the farm and people who didn't know how to point their feet, I was in front of the line. It seemed to me the most normal thing possible. I thought why not? I wasn't in touch with the issues of the time at all. I just enjoyed doing what I was used to doing in a much more conscious way. At the same time I was training like hell to do those things I couldn't do. When I started to make work a few years later, a broader range of movement possibilities were somehow made accessible. I feel very grateful for all of that because I don't feel at all that I have a revolutionary sensibility.

It may be true that neither critics nor audiences absorbed what happened in the sixties but I don't think I'd be doing what I'm doing now if that hadn't happened.

I've been thinking about the influences of other artists a lot lately—more than I ever have. Even wanting to begin to talk about people's work in those terms. I'm very interested in the overall energy or undertone of a work. Is there a positive or negative energy of a work? What are the generative forces of a piece of work? How is the energy being structured? I used to watch dancing like I watched people just walking on the street. Now I am more interested in the relationship of the performer to what he or she is doing.

Brown. The word "energy" throws me. It's one of those words like "vibes." It has no meaning for me. Are you talking about the humanness of the people?

Dunn. I'm talking about emphasis. Is there a craftsman-like approach, an inspirational approach, a hard-nosed approach, a consciously avant-garde approach to the work? What is coming to the fore?

Brown. I think that it comes into the category of naturalness or natural movements. Doing things in a straight way. The human way of doing something is often preferred when I give instructions to my performers to do something.

DON'T TELL ME WHO I AM

Rod Rodgers
1938–

Born in Cleveland Ohio and raised in Detroit, Rod Rodgers's *first teachers were his parents who impressed him with their long admiration for Katherine Dunham and Pearl Primus. Rodgers studied with devotees of Dunham, José Limón, and Hanya Holm before moving to New York to study and work with Mary Anthony, Erick Hawkins, Charles Weidman, and Holm herself. He credits early relationships/collaborations with musicians, designers, and extraordinary dancers as substantially determining the direction of his creative exploration.*

Established in 1968, the Rod Rodgers Dance Company boasts a repertoire of abstract, dance-drama, jazz, and modern dance works. It was one of the first American dance companies under the direction of an African-American artist to establish a base of recognition for something other than exclusively ethnic or traditional Afro-American styles.

Drawing from his background as a percussionist, Rodgers developed a signature series of Rhythmdances *in which the dancers make music-in-motion by playing hand-held instruments while they dance. In 1981, Rodgers began* Poets & Peacemakers, *a series of works inspired by the creative struggles of such African-American leaders as Langston Hughes, Harriet Tubman, and George Washington Carver. His 1997* Stance *continued his ongoing series of sculptural movement landscapes. Rod Rodgers also has choreographed for television and off-Broadway productions.*

"Don't Tell Me Who I Am," a succinct statement of purpose, first appeared in The Negro Digest.

(On several occasions I have been asked if I felt that my dance art is affected by my being Afro-American. This question surprises me because I am aware of the way my present work has evolved from my early experience and basic technique in Afro-Cuban and jazz dance. But in an art like dance, people have no way of seeing where you are coming from unless you have managed to retain examples of your early work in your repertoire, and I have not found this practical. So the question persists from blacks and whites who strongly feel that the most important thing a black artist can do today is to help establish a black cultural identity by emphasizing traditional Afro-American thematic material. The following statement from my point of view clarifies the role of non-traditional, experimental "black art.")

* * *

I am not looking for any over-simplified answer to the question: Who am I? It is obvious by now that I am not going to be a great white American dancer. But I have little patience with people who suggest that to be a black choreographer one must limit one's scope and deal exclusively with traditional Afro-American material.

The question of an artist's identity is one that he continually asks. He asks it through his chosen medium by experimentally probing into different aspects of his identity and environment. Whether one functions as a choreographer who also happens to be black, or as a black man who happens to be a choreographer is determined by one's point of view at a given moment. The ideal point of view at any given moment, for the individual artist, is the one which best allows him to create the most profoundly exciting art. If he cannot produce beautiful and exciting art, there is no point in discussing his political or ideological commitments in relation to art.

The militant black revolutionary may think of art in terms of the whole machinery of the revolution, as a means of bringing forth the rich heritage of the African in America and of creating a sense of identity for the sake of the revolution. Most of the existing dance companies which are instruments of black choreographers have placed their emphasis on traditional Afro-American material. They are exploring through their artistry the proud Afro-American heritage, and they can evoke poignant images which will encourage intolerance of racial suppression. But these images are not the only means of communicating a black consciousness. While traditional black art is playing a vital role in the awakening of a black cultural identity, now it is equally important for black artists to discourage the crystallization of new limiting stereotypes by not confining themselves to over-simplified traditional images.

I am not suggesting that black artists should or could cut themselves off from Afro-American tradition. Artist or layman, our past experience inevitably affects our articulation of present ideas. But if an artist's sense of immediacy is to vitalize his work, he should have freedom to decide which ideas he feels a need to communicate at a particular time. Artists have felt compelled to create images calling for social changes long before their own people were ready to initiate such changes. Other artists might never be moved to focus their art on socio-historic events. It is not a question of art for art's sake; it is a need to be true to one's own feelings. Although masterpieces *have* been created on commission, in the process of fulfilling some sponsor's vision, far more often the product of artists working with ideas which are devoid of deep personal relevance has tended to be poor art.

An artist's assumption that he knows exactly what his audience "needs" often results in art that is, at best, patronizing. The highest compliment an artist can pay his audience is to invite them to witness his exploration of the maximum possibilities of his art, based on his total experience.

The dance that I do is Afro-American, simply because I am Afro-American. My blackness is part of my identity as a human being, and my dance exploration is evolving in relation to my total experience as a man. It is simply a question of what takes precedence in the creative act: my total living experience, or those experiences which I consider particularly relevant to my blackness. Both white and black Americans have long been conditioned to accept the myth that Afro-Americans function well only in certain predictable areas. This myth must be dispelled. The refusal of black artists to confine their work to convenient categories will contribute to the destruction of this limited notion. Each dance that I create has grown out of my personal experience as a black American. Each movement that I explore is part of my own personal heritage.

My emphasis is on exploring through my medium, experimenting with dance, trying to find fresh ways of evoking physical and spiritual images to make new poetic comments about man's eternal beauty and pathos. My function in the revolution will be to share my personal experience—a vital and growing experience-through dance: it will not be to show only old stereotypes or create new ones.

TANK DIVE

Twyla Tharp
1941–

Twyla Tharp grew up in Southern California, where her
extracurricular activities included "baton, ballet, toe, flamenco,
drums, elocution, painting, viola, violin, acrobatics, shorthand,
German, and French." She graduated from Barnard College with a
degree in Art History, having crammed her courses between dance classes
in ballet, modern, and jazz. At the same time, Tharp often visited the
Dance Collection of The New York Public Library, searching for signs of
women artists. There, running her fingers over the images of Isadora
Duncan, Mary Wigman, Doris Humphrey, Ruth St. Denis, and Martha
Graham, she "tried to absorb their power and authority"—their potency.

Tharp made her professional debut with the Paul Taylor Dance
Company in 1963 in a role that consisted entirely of "one unlit
upstage crossover, a crablike crawl . . . performed underneath a huge
striped beach towel." By then she already "differentiated between those
who rendered the work of others, . . . and those who did their own
work." She felt she had to follow the advice Ruth St. Denis had given
to Martha Graham when she had no dance to show. "Well, dear, go
out and get one." The following excerpt from Tharp's 1992 autobiography Push Comes to Shove, describes the search for, creation, and
performance of Tharp's first dance.

In 1965, Twyla Tharp founded her first company which she has
sustained in various forms (and with one brief hiatus) every since.
Building on her foundation of "the right angle, the diagonal, the spiral, and the circle," she went on to develop a distinctive style known for
its blending of more traditional training with idiosyncratic gestures, clear
structure, and consistent entertainment. Twyla Tharp has created over
70 works for her own company, various other ballet and modern companies, Broadway shows and film.

I started to work on my first concert, anguishing over the question "What is dancing?" I allowed myself only one assumption: dance is movement in space and time. The space was a small Bauhaus auditorium, Room 1604, belonging to the Hunter College art department, where Bob [Bob Huot] worked as an instructor. The structure of my work utilized the curvy walls, balcony, and small stage of the place. The entire evening—April 29, 1965—lasted seven minutes. Any stragglers missed the whole thing. Seven minutes was all I could handle and about all I had to say. It would be enough to test the waters.

Having accounted for time and space, all I needed was a beginning, a middle, and an end. I began in the dark with almost nothing, "a radio beginning" as I like to think of it, entering upstage of the audience. The ending was face down, in a blackout, an homage to death: how else to end definitively? Then all I needed was the middle, a way of getting from the beginning to death as directly and economically as possible. But how could I select from the infinite number of choices to make a middle? The solution was to decide what couldn't be eliminated.

My answer was the right angle, the diagonal, the spiral, and the circle. These are the basis of all movement; everything else moves in patterns through a combination of these four. Fine, but how to make this dramatic? I figured I'd better couch my diagonals and spirals in sex and surprise if I wanted to reach an audience.

Sex was—when the lights came on—myself in a backless leotard cut high on the sides with red pants, slightly bell-bottomed but tight at the hip, stopping short to reveal ankles in velvet high-heeled bedroom slippers.

The surprise was a real shocker: circling my right arm one time, a full three hundred and sixty degrees in a plane parallel to my body, I snapped a yo-yo down to sleep, then brought it up. Perfecting this move required hours of practice. I think I left it in because I needed something real to worry about, distracting me from the inevitable opening-night nerves.

O.K., what next? I stepped out of the bedroom slippers and into a pair of large, skilike wooden shoes. I stretched my back

first into a right angle, then reached farther out onto the diagonal–like a skier soaring off a slope, free, out into space. Then I
left these shoes, went onto the stage, and held a relevé in second position, the arms reaching diagonally out from the shoulders, spread-eagled. The double diagonal, the X, Leonardo's
Vitruvian man. All three minutes of Petula Clark's song
"Downtown" played and I did not move, except to rotate the
X once, ninety degrees in space, to reveal the form in profile.
Blackout.

Part Two extended the diagonal farther out in space. Two
couples (one including Bob Huot) came together onstage,
rushed down a set of stairs in the middle of the apron, then
spread out and exited diagonally, the same side they'd come
from. The X of my vertical relevé moved into horizontal space.
Blackout.

Part Three was spirals and curves. Changing costumes during Part Two to a white cap, fencing jacket, and tights, I raced
down the stage steps, caught hold of a subway pole, spun
around it, executed a baseball slide just above the ground, then
hit the deck—splat!—sprawling forward on my face, taking the
weight through the backs of my wrists, spread-eagled once
more, though now face down, an homage to dance icons after
a long apprenticeship, and a reference to the bows that end all
well-taught ballet classes, a moment of reverence as the students
both acknowledge the instructor and begin to practice an
action they will need to make as performers before an audience. The curtain call was embedded in the dance. I wanted to
connect my first choreographic effort with the end of my class-
work, to show my dance as an extension of my lessons, not a
departure from them. This content was prompted by both loy-
alty and pragmatism: it has always seemed to me that there's a
better chance for a future where there has been a past. Blackout
and clear. There was no acknowledgment of the audience.

Tank Dive: the title referred to my sense that my chances of
succeeding as a choreographer like Graham, Balanchine, or
Cunningham were the same as someone diving off a forty-foot
platform into a teacup of water or, better yet, from a very high
platform, about nine hundred thousand feet up, into a thim-

bleful of water. It was not a solo concert but a full-fledged event, a complete production. Bob Huot designed the fliers, props, and wardrobe; my friend Jennifer Tipton lit the piece. I did the necessaries: sewed, got mailing lists, took announcements to the printer, addressed and stamped, tried to get press coverage—everything to assure that my efforts would not go unnoticed. I didn't promote myself as a star. I had always seen myself as a star: I wanted to be a galaxy.

The next morning, I raced from the Franklin Street loft to West Fourth Street for the early editions of the *Times* and the *Post*. Waiting for the newsstand attendant to give me my change, I felt as though I were holding my breath for final grades. Not thinking it classy to paw through the papers on a street corner, I went into the nearest Chock Full O'Nuts. I ordered a coffee and a powdered-sugar doughnut. Then I looked for the reviews. Nothing. In either paper. *Nothing.* Did I have the right papers— May 1, 1965? I couldn't believe the critics didn't realize what we had here was history created last night.

The moment was a real crisis of confidence and taught me an important lesson: if you want to create art, you'd best have a deep belief in yourself and no ulterior motives. Today I'm grateful for the relative obscurity of my first five years as a choreographer. I had time to develop my own backbone, to find what I deemed important without having to cater to public taste, so that when reaction finally came—both negative and positive (for they can be equally misleading)—I was well grounded. There was no financial remuneration and little attention paid me those first five years; so I simply went on asking myself, "Do you want to do this or don't you?" Today I try to keep both money and celebrity from standing in the way of asking this same question every day.

Part Five

THE
NEW VISION

INTRODUCTION

by
Don McDonagh

The transitional decade of the seventies, which spawned few new creative directions, was for the most part a time of consolidation and expansion for sixties choreographers who started from a basically minimalist orientation. Each developed some aspect of this austere but fruitful area. Simone Forti and Yvonne Rainer published major texts outlining their aesthetic beliefs. Rainer subsequently abandoned the stage to work as a filmmaker while Forti continued to find creative challenges in harnassing everyday gesture or even animal movement. Steve Paxton established the contact improvisation movement, Laura Dean and Lucinda Childs pursued their efficient and emotionally-muted work in more traditional performance spaces. The theatrically inclined Meredith Monk and Twyla Tharp had little difficulty in effectively restaging their alternative space spectacles for proscenium stages.

The choreographers of the eighties and nineties who followed the minimalist revolution were freed from the inherited regimentation that minimalists had felt compelled to reject in their search for expressive freedom. There were seemingly no rules left to be broken. The necessity of rigorously trained technique had been bypassed. The musical forms considered so necessary for thematic development had been flouted by using non-rhythmic sound or silence. Character-establishing costuming had been discarded, sometimes in favor of nudity; and sanctioned performing spaces had been spurned for gymnasiums, open fields or even rooftops. By the end of the seventies there was nowhere left to go in stripping away traditional practices.

The generation of the eighties and nineties began to work with new, non-conventional forms of theatrical presentation, as had Pilobolus which preceded them in the seventies. The latter continued to create works that did not require dance training, but emphasized highly skilled, gymnastic bodily control. With similar emphasis on physicality, Molissa Fenley turned high energy aerobics into a dance form. Other choreographers shaped tumbling and aerial acrobatics into spectator spectacles or appropriated elements of sport for aesthetic ends. The human voice reciting narrative or descriptive material at times became an accompanying sound for dances.

A rainbow range of sexual expression formed thematic material for making dances. These included gender ambiguity, characterized by cross-dressing and same sex emotional involvements. Mark Morris casually subverted the customary male/female roles by assigning non-traditional behavior patterns to the opposite sex. His cross-dressing corps de ballet in the Snowflakes waltz in *The Hard Nut* (his settings of *The Nutcracker*) was an outrageously amusing spoof of ballet choreographic and costuming conventions. The subject of sexual desire which had been guardedly alluded to in previous generations, from Loïe Fuller at the turn-of-the-century to Trisha Brown in the second half-of-the-century, became an erotic boutique in the the eighties and nineties.

Extreme self-concern regarding freedom in personal and all institutional relations, celebrated in the revolutionary sixties, continued to engage this generation. However, accompanying this self-involvement was an extreme skepticism regarding the stability of emotional commitment between individuals. The mistrust of traditional institutions, both in public and private life, that was overtly proclaimed in the Judson generation's work, had become a form of received pessimistic wisdom among the succeeding generation of choreographers.

Some dances depicted anguished, ambiguous activities: frustrated effort, punishment, struggle, and awkward stress. Eiko and Koma were among several performers who created mood pieces of isolation and mystery revealed in extremely slow-moving passages. By contrast, a muted background note of happy, unconcerned self-involvement was sounded by others who used dance movement with an easy flippancy to convey their own humorously hedonistic explorations of life situations. Some choreographers combined moving or still projected images with live performance, as rapidly developing technical advances opened new creative possibilities.

The theater setting with its implicit convention of narrative construction was re-invigorated by choreographers who were willing to use its evocative space but not always its rigid linear conventions. The ambiance of the theater, with its promise of entertainment and creative communication, had been found congenial once again after the austerities of the sixties revolution.

A PASSION
FOR MUSIC

Mark Morris
1956–

Born in Seattle, Washington, Mark Morris saw a José Greco
show when he was eight and fell in love with flamenco dance.
By 13, he had joined the Koleda Balkan Dance Ensemble
whose repertoire and spirit of dancing greatly influenced his later work.

Mark Morris arrived in New York when he was 19 and was hired
by the Eliot Feld Ballet almost immediately. For seven years, he performed with an eclectic array of companies, always knowing that he
would create his own work.

The Mark Morris Dance Group gave its first concert in 1980 in
Merce Cunningham's studio, a space often rented by self-presenting
artists. From 1988-1991, Mark Morris served as Director of Dance
at the Théâtre Royal de la Monnaie in Brussels, the national opera
house of Belgium. During this period, he created many new dances
including three evening-length works: The Hard Nut (his comic
book-inspired version of The Nutcracker), L'Allegro, il Penseroso
ed il Moderato, and Dido and Aeneas.

Since 1980, Morris has created over 90 works for the Dance Group,
as well as choreographing for ballet companies and opera. He co-founded
the White Oak Dance Project with Mikhail Baryshnikov, choreographed
and directed various opera productions, and completed film projects including a collaboration with cellist Yo-Yo Ma entited Falling Down Stairs.

Noted for his musicality, movement versatility, and craft, Morris is
often proclaimed to be heir apparent to Doris Humphrey or George
Balanchine. His devotion to music becomes clear in the following
excerpt from a 1992 interview.

Thea Singer (TS): I would consider you a classicist because of your adherence to structure and because your work springs right from the music. Do you agree?

Mark Morris (MM): Yeah.

TS: That's how you would classify yourself?

MM: I wouldn't classify myself, but I would agree with you if you classified me that way.

TS: What if I classified you some other way?

MM: It's fine. I wouldn't agree with you, but you could do it.

TS: Why do you agree with "classicist?"

MM: I would say because I'm concerned with—corny as this is—truth and beauty and proportion. That's what makes me a classical mind.

TS: What do you mean by proportion?

MM: Classical proportion. Something that's long and short. Structures. Whether there's geometry or tempo or traffic or anything. Just the overall conceit of a piece has to be perfectly well constructed for me to enjoy working on it. That's a classical symptom. . . .

TS: You once told me that you're interested in music and you're a choreographer rather than that you're interested in dancing and you're a choreographer. Can you talk about that?

MM: Music is to me generally more interesting and of higher quality than dance shows are. So I approach it from that angle, as a musician. . . .

TS: What do you mean by "more interesting?"

MM: More rigorous, more satisfying. I think it's usually at a higher level of proficiency and often taste. So interesting in every way.

TS: Behemoth is the only piece you've made to silence, right?

MM: The only piece that I've made to silence that we have performed to no music. I sometimes work with no music. But then we do it with music.

TS: I thought that you usually started from the score.

MM: I do, usually. But sometimes if I'm working on a particular effect, then I work often for days without music, or weeks without music. I did a lot of *Strict Songs* [performed to Lou Harrison] without music. . . .

TS: When I talked to you previously you mentioned that you found certain kinesthetic experiences "exhilarating and thought-provoking." What falls into that realm?

MM: I know that I get a giant kinesthetic thrill from people singing, more than I usually get from watching people dancing. It's something that very occasionally happens in opera if everything is great. I get a particular sort of charge that I don't get from just about anything else. So that's one reason that I work with a lot of vocal music, and then that charges the dancing in a way that I don't think can be achieved as well with unfortunate taped music.

TS: Do you get that thrill from watching your dancers do your dances?

MM: Sometimes, yeah. When I forget that I made it up, and I'm just watching it and I think, "Wow. How do you do that?"

TS: . . . How would you explain your facility with music?

MM: . . . I read music. I can read anything. I read scores. And I can play things on the piano, though I'm not a pianist. And I'm not a singer but I can sing. I learned how to read music very young from my father.

TS: How old were you?

MM: I was probably six or seven. And I improvised on the piano for a long time, though when I finally took lessons I couldn't stand it. And I sang in choruses, I studied music theory in high school. I had a fabulous music-theory course in high school, and I mostly listen to a lot of stuff and read about it. It's my interest, it's my passion. . . .

TS: What is it that you love so much about Baroque music?

MM: Well, it's fabulous, isn't it? One thing is that all of these rhythms are dance rhythms, the French suites and stuff. You can break it down into all of these things, into the passepied and the bourrée and the gavotte and the gigue. And that's real. That's the tempo of these things, it's how they're supposed to be played and that's how they're constructed. And you're supposed to dance to that music.

TS: Who's your favorite composer?

MM: Bach.

TS: Second favorite.

MM: Then that gets complicated. Bach is number one. As I've said, Bach is God's favorite composer, too. And I like Handel a great deal. I like a lot of people, but Bach is like another category because Bach is divine in the literal sense.

TS: Have you played Bach on the piano yourself?

MM: Yeah, badly and slowly.

TS: You've created more than 60 dances in 10 years.

MM: I can't stop. That's what I like to do. I like to make up new dances.

TS: You're not getting tired?

MM: Oh, of course I'm tired all the time. But I learn stuff and then I want to make up another dance.

TS: Where do they all come from?

MM: Brain. I make them up. I start with nobody doing anything and then pretty soon people are doing things and it's a dance eventually. . . .

TS: What do you want the audience to get out of watching your dances?

MM: I don't care. I hope they enjoy watching them. I like that a performance be entertaining. And I have no lessons to teach to anybody. That's not my business. . . .

TS: You've been touted as the "heir apparent to the great moderns." What do you do with that?

MM: Well, I think some of the great moderns weren't so great.

TS: Do you think that those were the ones they meant when they made that comment?

MM: [Laughs.] Yeah, maybe. I don't know. The great moderns—Isadora Duncan, Doris Humphrey, Martha Graham, maybe. Those are moderns.

TS: And then Mark Morris.

MM: Well, there are other things in between.

TS: Well, how does that feel?

MM: It's fine. It pleases me. It's nice. It's a lovely compliment. I didn't say it. It's fine with me. I certainly think I do good work, but I'm also not interested in revealing the truth of the past, you know, like, "Wasn't dancing great then?" I don't feel like that. [Laughs.] Because chances are it wasn't. Who knows? We see these beautiful pictures, as if that is modern dance. No it's not. It's a good picture.

TS: What about your being called "the most musical choreographer since Balanchine?"

MM: That's probably true.

TS: You say that in such an unassuming way.

MM: I mean, who is? Merce is, but it's not in a way that we can follow. I think that means that I do dancing to music and you can see how it works. And whether that is, as some people say, "Disney-esque," that doesn't matter because that's a lovely compliment to me because Disney was a great choreographer.... It's like, "Oh, wow, this is fantastic music and here's what's happening to it and it's just as I imagined." Of course, you never imagined that. You see it and you think you did. So it's obvious....

.... And also, if it wasn't beneath Mr. Mozart's dignity to repeat something exactly, it's certainly not beneath mine. It's even more pretentious to assume that [the repetition] isn't meant. Or people laugh because it's surprising. It's like, come one. You know, this figure happens four times and this figure in the choreography happens four times. Wow, isn't it a miracle. So that's seen as obvious or whatever. I don't have to do that, I choose to. It's not an accident.

TS: Whom would you point to as influences?

MM: I don't know. Because it's broad. It's basically everything I do all the time. It's like what I listen to or who I spend time with, what movies I see or books I read. I don't search for inspiration.

TS: So you wouldn't say there are any choreographers that you . . .

MM: There are choreographers whose work I love and think is great, but I don't necessarily want to emulate them. I have thought very highly of Mr. Taylor's work for years. That doesn't mean I love every dance. It means that he has a personal aesthetic that I find intriguing and always, usually, enjoyable. People accuse me, because I work with Baroque music, of being allied somehow with Mr. Taylor, which is not at all true. And I would hesitate before saying that he's very musical. He uses some good music sometimes, but if you really look at the dances, it doesn't read that way to me at all. Which is of course the exact opposite of Mr. Balanchine's where if you watch these works fresh, and it's the only way you can because they're such fantastic creations, then you have to see that that is *obvious.* It's like, "Of course this should happen at this moment." And it's profoundly musical and profoundly spiritual, and I think that's lacking in most choreography. I don't want my experience at the theater to be the same one I had on the subway coming to the theater. Or waiting in line at unemployment. I don't want that. I want something else.

TS: So I'd imagine that you attend a lot more music than dance.

MM: I see more dance than I say I do, and I hear less music than I would like to. I don't go out a lot.

Post-modernism?

Although most of the authors in the following selections began dancing either in more traditional modern dance or in the Judson Dance Theater of the 1960s, each has found a unique voice and developed a singular approach to choreography. The term "post-modern" has been used to describe this development, as if it were a replacement for "modern." Actually, it may be seen as another stage in the ongoing evolution of modern dance.

Mary Fulkerson, earned degrees from the University of Illinois before working as a creative associate at the University of Buffalo. Having studied with Ruth Currier (a Limón/Humphrey dancer) and at the Cunningham Studio, she went on to incorporate a "release" and imagery approach into her work. Teaching and choreographing mostly in Dartington College of Arts and the School for New Dance Development (a department of Amsterdam's Theatre School), Fulkerson explores three major concerns: anatomy, kinetics, and choreography. She is considered a seminal figure in British New Dance and aligns herself with post-modern dance.

The presentation of ordered works where a particular viewpoint is expressed, or where thematic concerns prevail, has its fulfillment within the concerns of the modernists. Such works seek to fulfill our expectations of performance and craftsmanship and lead us throughout to intended realizations which are the same as those of the creators of such works.

The presentation of fields of experience, of complex and unformed information, of bits and pieces, of textures, is the concern of post-modern work. Such works seek to leave us with questions as they do not lead each member of the audience to the same understandings. In the minds of creators of such works there is no such one apparent meaning.

Modern works seek to *show,* to *communicate something,* to

transcend real life. Post-modern works seek to be, to question the textures and complexities of real life.

* * *

*Born in the United States, **Molissa Fenley** spent most of her child-hood in Nigeria, where she witnessed traditional shamanic ritual and dancing. She returned to the United States in 1971 to attend Mills College, from which she graduated in 1975. Fenley formed her own company in 1977, but decided to work as a solo artist in 1988. She is known for her austere, intensely physical style.*

The whole dance experience for me is extremely sacred and ritualistic, as well as all-consuming. From the moment I wake up until the time I go to bed, I'm involved with the idea that the language of communication between the body and the mind is what my dancing is about. Since I started working as a soloist, it's become even more clear that the transmission of an idea into purity of action is absolutely a straight line; there's no translation from one to the other. . . .

. . . What I try to bring home to people is that you can only experience something with your own perceptions. When I'm on tour, visiting high schools, for instance, invariably at the beginning, there's whispering and catcalling and that sort of thing. Before I start talking to them, I dance one dance. Then I start talking. Then I dance a few more dances. I tell them, look at this work as the bridge between you and me, not between you and your friends, not between you and what your mother thinks, or anything like that; just you and me. Think of that bridge as a direct line into your inner life. Not you and me, just you into yourself.

Cross that bridge, cross that threshold, and what happens? It's really interesting, because we don't know how to do that as a culture. Instead, it's always camaraderie, group orientation. I think people who walk alone can understand more than peo-ple who walk together. You can walk together after you've done some walking alone.

* * *

Bill T. Jones *entered college as an athlete and actor, and emerged from
the State University of New York at Binghamton with dance training
under his belt. He formed Bill T. Jones/Arnie Zane & Company (now
Bill T. Jones/Arnie Zane Dance Company) in 1982 and went on to
create such works as* Uncle Tom's Cabin; Fever Swamp; *and*
Still/Here, *a choreographic exploration of AIDS.*

. . . I always feel, whenever I am on stage, that it is a place for
transformations. I feel it's almost a mystical place, therefore I am
allowed to stretch and do all sorts of things which are ritualistic and because of the context can be shocking. I can say things
that I would not normally say. I try to open the gates to the
subconscious in what I say and what I am doing. . . .

* * *

David Gordon *performed in the companies of James Waring and Yvonne
Rainer in the 1960s. He showed work in the first Judson Church performance and was a founding member of the improvisational ensemble,
Grand Union. Gordon has created work for his own Pick Up Company,
off-Broadway productions such as* Shleimiel the First, *and video.*

David Gordon: I think that what every improvisational group
needs is a very intelligent madman. And that's the person who
can throw extraordinary curves into what can result in a kind
of introspective, banal, self-perpetuating involvement.

Interviewer: Like an unleader. . . .

David Gordon: Somebody who just turns the place upside
down by his craziness. I thought for awhile that if you were to
break down the Grand Union into who I thought was what, I
thought I was the madman. But what I find is that my eccen-
tricities are really dominated by a kind of logic and what you
really need is somebody who is illogical, whose eccentricity
cannot be predicted.

* * *

Garth Fagan *left his native Jamaica to tour with Ivy Baxter and the
Jamaican National Dance Company. Counting Pearl Primus, Lavinia
Williams, Martha Graham, José Limón, Mary Hinkson and Alvin*

*Ailey as major influences, Fagan forged his own dance language includ-
ing aspects of modern, Afro-Caribbean, and post-modern dance. He
choreographs for his own company, Garth Fagan Dance (formed in 1970
in Rochester, New York) as well as on and off Broadway and in opera.*

I have to have the dream to keep plugging with my aesthetic,
which is against the grain because, first, it involves African-
Caribbean textures, which are not understood in the American
mainstream; and second, I have a penchant for jazz and jazz
rhythms which are also maligned in America—certainly in
comparison to the response in Europe or Japan. There are not
that many jazz stations on the air, for instance. Jazz concerts
don't sell out the way rock concerts or country-and-western
concerts do.

And the dance critics have a hideously old-fashioned concept of jazz dance where you swivel your hips and get sexy—
and that's jazz. But it's a complex improvisatory art form, rich
in counterpoint, rich in texture. If you look around in the theater every night when we perform, you see lots of jazz greats
sitting there. They love the work.

* * *

*Lucinda Childs began her career as a choreographer and performer in
1963 as an original member of the Judson Dance Theater. She formed
her own company in 1973 and, since 1979, has collaborated with a
number of composers and designers on a series of large-scale, full-length
productions, including the opera* Einstein on the Beach.

Interviewer: Thinking back to the Judson Church period and
your radical choreographic agenda of those years, what do you
feel you subsequently discarded? Conversely, are there principles
which you rejected back then but now embrace in your work?

Lucinda Childs: I think I've discarded the use of the pedestrian
vocabulary, that is to say, the vocabulary which was utilized
during the period of the Judson when we were conscientious-
ly trying to avoid anything that could be associated with the
traditional vocabulary of dance. This was a conceptual idea and
an interesting exercise but I discarded it in the early seventies—

in the late sixties, as a matter of fact—in the interest of going back to the studio and dealing with drawn movement. And through that process I built my vocabulary back up to be consistent, in terms of content, with what you'd find in a fairly normal dance vocabulary but, in terms of dynamic, entirely different, I think.

* * *

Eiko and Koma, originally from Tokyo, dropped out of college around 1970, met in a Butoh dance class, and studied with Kazuo Ohno and Tatsumi Hijikata (central figures in the Japanese avant-garde theatrical movement of the 1960s) and Manja Chmiel (a disciple of Mary Wigman). They are self-described "slow workers" in the choreographic process, having developed an evocative style that includes extremely slow motion and nudity. Eiko and Koma use only their first names in order to be as stripped-down and simple as possible.

Interviewer: When you start to make a piece do you start from an idea and then the movement evolves from that?

Eiko: Right, right, we don't make the piece to show the technique, and if we don't have to move for the piece then we don't move.

Interviewer: How set are your performances?

Koma: The structure is set, but movement wise as we don't dance with music, also we don't count, there is quite a lot of freedom, but I don't like just free improvisation.

Interviewer: There was a great intensity in some parts of your performance. How do you generate this?

Eiko: What I usually do through the work process is have enough energy inside before coming up with the movement. So we don't do hash movement for the sake of hash movement.

Interviewer: It gives a real power so people are really waiting for what's going to happen next.

Eiko: Another reason is I take enough time so it becomes obvious what to expect next and it becomes a communal affair rather than a personal thing.

* * *

Deborah Hay's performances and choreography explore the nature of experience, perception and attention. She was a founding member of the Judson Dance Theater and a member of the Merce Cunningham Company in the mid-sixties. Since 1970 she has worked independently. In an ongoing campaign to educate and create new audiences for her work, Hay has written several books about her work and approach to dance.

Since 1970, my practice and resources as a dancer and choreographer have shifted from physical to perceptual challenges. I perceive the doing of movement as rhetorical. Every dancer has just so much physical prowess, so much personal experience shaping his/her movement vocabulary. However, if one imaginatively endows every cell in one's body with an individual intelligence for movement perception, the experience of movement increases exponentially. Performance becomes a continuum of multiple cellular experiences unfolding simultaneously. One can only be at the feet of one's body as a teacher—not the teacher instructing the body how to dance! The lessons learned here are as untranslatable as they are blunt. The wisdom of my body, when it is invested with individuated cellular perception, is hilariously profound. What I am doing when I am dancing is directing my attention to the validity of these tiny intelligences and reflecting that information back to the world. This is what I call the performance of dancing. It is an on-going manifestation of mystery. It is the unknown brought to light for an instant. For myself and the audience.

* * *

*Born and raised in racially segregated Kansas City, **Jowale Willa Jo Zollar** didn't discover white American modern dance until she entered college. She earned an undergraduate degree from the University of Missouri and an MFA from Florida State University (where she also taught for two years). Founded in New York in 1985, her performing ensemble, Urban Bush Women, integrates contemporary dance experimentation, the ritualistic abandon of the Afro-American dance tradition, and the influences of jazz and black folk art.*

Interviewer: How useful do you find experimental post-modernism for expressing the black experience?

Jowale Willa Jo Zollar: I think anything is valid for expressing any experience. You find your form of expression and if you're inclined towards post-modernism, then that may work for you, whether you're Black, Asian. . . .

Interviewer: So it's just a tool?

Jowale Willa Jo Zollar: Yeah, it's a tool.

Interviewer: There's nothing particularly about the challenge, the rebellion?

Jowale Willa Jo Zollar: Not for me. For the people who were involved in the beginning of the post-modern scene—maybe that's where they were more coming from. I guess I'm reaping the benefits from it.

Interviewer: . . . So, you're picking up on a tradition that was already laid: the rebellion?

Jowale Willa Jo Zollar: Well, all the traditions: I feel everything, from Alvin Ailey, Katherine Dunham, Pearl Primus, Steve Paxton, all those people laid ground work in some way or another, which makes it easier for the next artist to work, even if you rebel against what they did—it still makes it easier for you to work.

SELECTED
BIBLIOGRAPHY

I Artists

Isadora Duncan

Daly, Ann. *Done into Dance: Isadora Duncan in America.* Bloomington: Indiana University Press, 1995.

Duncan, Irma. *Duncan Dancer.* Middletown, CT: Wesleyan University Press, 1966.

———. *Isadora Duncan: Pioneer in the Art of Dance.* New York: The New York Public Library, 1958.

———. *The Technique of Isadora Duncan.* New York: Kamin Publishers, 1937. Reprint. Brooklyn: Dance Horizons, 1970.

Duncan, Isadora. *The Art of the Dance.* New York: Theatre Arts Books, 1970.

———. *My Life.* New York: Boni & Liveright, 1927. Reprint. New York: Liveright, 1955.

Desti, Mary. *The Untold Story: The Life of Isadora Duncan 1921–1927.* New York: Horace Liveright, 1929; Reprint, with new preface by Dale Harris. New York: Da Capo Press, 1981.

Levien, Julia. *Duncan Dance: A Guide for Young People Ages Six to Sixteen.* Pennington, NJ: Princeton Book Company, 1994.

Loewenthal, Lillian. *The Search for Isadora: The Legend & Legacy of Isadora Duncan.* Pennington, NJ: Princeton Book Company, 1993.

MacDougall, Allan Ross. *Isadora: A Revolutionary in Art and Love.* New York: Thomas Nelson & Sons, 1960.

Magriel, Paul David. *Isadora Duncan.* New York: Henry Holt & Co., 1947.

Maria-Theresa. "The Spirit of Isadora Duncan." In Myron Howard Nadel and Constance Gwen Nadel, eds., *The Dance Experience: Readings in Dance Appreciation.* New York: Praeger Publishers, 1970.

McVay, Gordon. *Isadora and Esenin: The Story of Isadora Duncan and Sergei Esenin.* Ann Arbor, MI: Ardis, 1980.

Roslavleva, Natalia. "Prechistenka 20: The Isadora Duncan School in Moscow." *Dance Perspectives* 64 (1975).

Sandomir, Larry. *Isadora Duncan: Revolutionary Dancer.* Austin, TX: Raintree Steck-Vaughn, 1995.

Schneider, Ilya ilyich. *Isadora Duncan: The Russian Years.* Translated by David Magershack. London: MacDonald, 1968.

Seroff, Victor. *The Real Isadora.* London: Hutchinson, 1972.

Sorell, Walter. "Two Rebels, Two Giants: Isadora and Martha." In Walter Sorell, ed., *The Dance Has Many Faces.* 2d ed. rev. New York: Columbia University Press, 1966.

Steegmuller, Francis, ed. *Your Isadora: The Love Story of Isadora Duncan and Gordon Craig.* New York: Random House and The New York Public Library, 1974.

Terry, Walter. *Isadora Duncan: Her Life, Her Art, Her Legacy.* New York: Dodd, Mead & Co., 1963.

———. "The Legacy of Isadora Duncan and Ruth St. Denis." *Dance Perspectives* 5 (1960).

Loïe Fuller

Ault, Thomas C. "La Loïe Fuller: Pioneer in Dance Lighting and Effects." *Dance Teacher Now* 5, no. 3 (May–June 1983): 13–16.

Current, Richard Nelson and Marcia Ewing Current. *Loïe Fuller: Goddess of Light.* Boston, MA: Northeastern University Press, 1997.

DeMorini, Claire. "Loïe Fuller, The Fairy of Light." In Paul Magriel, ed., *Chronicles of American Dance.* New York: Henry Holt & Co., 1948.

Fuller, Loïe. *Fifteen Years of a Dancer's Life.* Boston: Small, Maynard & Co., 1913. Reprint. Brooklyn: Dance Horizons, 1976.

Kermode, Frank. "Loïe Fuller and the Dance Before Diaghilev." *Theatre Arts* 46, no. 9 (1962): 6–21.

Sommer, Sally R. "Loïe Fuller's Art of Music and Light." *Dance Chronicle* 4, no. 4 (1982): 389–401.

West, Martha Ullman. "Fuller, Rosenthal & Tipton: The Light Fantastic." *Dance Magazine* (Feb. 1996): 88–92.

Ruth St. Denis

St. Denis, Ruth, and Shawn, Ted. *Denishawn Magazine* 1–3 (1924–1925).

———. *Lotus Light.* Boston and New York: Houghton, Mifflin & Co., 1932.

———. "Religious Manifestations in the Dance." In Walter Sorell, ed., *The Dance Has Many Faces.* 2d ed. rev. New York: Columbia University Press, 1966.

———. *An Unfinished Life.* New York and London: Harper & Bros., 1939. Reprint. Brooklyn: Dance Horizons, 1969.

Schlundt, Christena. "Into the Mystic with Miss Ruth." *Dance Perspectives* 47 (1971).

———. *The Professional Appearances of Ruth St. Denis and Ted Shawn.* New York: The New York Public Library, 1962.

Shawn, Ted. *Ruth St. Denis.* San Francisco: J. H. Nash, 1920.

Shelton, Suzanne. *Divine Dancer: A Biography of Ruth St. Denis.* Garden City, NY: Doubleday, 1981.

Sherman, Jane. *Denishawn: The Enduring Influence.* Boston: Twayne Pub., 1983.

———. *The Drama of Denishawn Dance.* Middletown, CT: Wesleyan University Press, 1979.

———. *Soaring: The Diary and Letters of a Denishawn Dancer in the Far East, 1925–1926.* Middletown, CT: Wesleyan University Press, 1976.

Terry, Walter. "The Legacy of Isadora Duncan and Ruth St. Denis." *Dance Perspectives* 5 (1960).

———. *Miss Ruth: The More Living Life of Ruth St. Denis.* New York: Dodd, Mead & Co., 1969.

Ted Shawn

Dreier, Katherine Sophie. *Shawn the Dancer.* London: I. M. Dent & Son, Ltd., 1933.

Schlundt, Christena. *The Professional Appearances of Ruth St. Denis and Ted Shawn.* New York: The New York Public Library, 1962.

———. *The Professional Appearances of Ted Shawn and His Men Dancers.* New York: The New York Public Library, 1967.

Shawn, Ted. *The American Ballet.* New York: Henry Holt & Co., 1926.

———. *Dance We Must.* Pittsfield, MA: Eagle Printing & Binding Co., 1940, 1950, 1963. Reprint. New York: Haskell House, 1974.

———. *Every Little Movement.* Pittsfield, MA: Eagle Printing & Binding Co., 1954, 1963. Reprint. Brooklyn: Dance Horizons, 1968.

———. *One Thousand and One Night Stands.* With Gray Poole. New York: Doubleday, 1960.

———. *Ruth St. Denis.* San Francisco: J. H. Nash, 1920.

———. *33 Years of American Dance.* Pittsfield, MA: Eagle Printing & Binding A Cappella 1959.

Sherman, Jane. "The American Indian Imagery of Ted Shawn." *Attitude* 9, no. 1 (Winter 1993): 17–21.

Sherman, Jane and Barton Mumaw. *Barton Mumaw, Dancer: from Denishawn to Jacob's Pillow and Beyond.* Brooklyn: Dance Horizons, 1986.

———. "How it all began: Ted Shawn's First Modern All-Male Dance Concert." *Dance Magazine* (July 1982): 42–46.

Terry, Walter. *Ted Shawn: Father of American Dance.* New York: Dial Press, 1977.

Mary Wigman

Holm, Hanya. "The Mary Wigman I Know." In Walter Sorell, ed., *The Dance Has Many Faces*. 2d ed. rev. New York: Columbia University Press, 1966.

Manning, Susan. *Ecstasy and the Demon: Feminism and Nationalism in the dances of Mary Wigman*. Berkeley: University of California Press, 1993.

Partsch-Bergsohn, Isa. "Laban: Magic and Science as Seen by Mary Wigman and Kurt Jooss." *Dance Theatre Journal* 4, no. 3 (Autumn 1986): 15–16.

Scheyer, Ernst. "The Shape of Space: The Art of Mary Wigman and Oskar Schlemmer." *Dance Perspectives* 41(1970).

Wigman, Mary. *The Language of Dance*. Translated by Walter Sorell. Middletown, CT: Wesleyan University Press, 1966.

——. *The Mary Wigman Book*. Edited and translated by Walter Sorell. Middletown, CT: Wesleyan University Press, 1975.

——. "The New German Dance." In Virginia Stewart and Merle Armitage, eds., *The Modern Dance*. New York: E. Weyhe, 1935. Reprint. Brooklyn: Dance Horizons, 1970.

——. "The Philosophy of Modern Dance." In Selma Jeanne Cohen, ed., *Dance as a Theatre Art*. 2d ed. Pennington, NJ: Princeton Book Company, 1992.

Martha Graham

Anderson, Jack. "Some Personal Grumbles About Martha Graham." *Ballet Review* 2, no. 1 (1967): 25.

Armitage, Merle, ed. *Martha Graham*. Los Angeles: privately printed, 1937. Reprint. Brooklyn: Dance Horizons, 1966.

Borek, Tom. "Graham." *Eddy* 4 (1974): 28–37.

De Mille, Agnes. *Martha: The Life and Work of Martha Graham*. New York: Random House, 1991.

Dudley, Jane. "The Early Life of an American Modern Dancer." *Dance Research* 10, no. 1 (Spring 1992): 3–20.

Graham, Martha. "The American Dance." In Virginia Stewart and Merle Armitage, eds., *The Modern Dance*. New York: E. Weyhe, 1935. Reprint. Brooklyn: Dance Horizons, 1970.

——. *Blood Memory*. New York: Doubleday, 1991.

——. "A Dancer's World." *Dance Observer* 25, no. 1 (1958): 5.

——. "How I Became a Dancer." In Myron Howard Nadel and Constance Gwen Nadel, eds., *The Dance Experience: Readings in Dance Appreciation*. New York: Praeger Publishers, 1970.

——. "Martha Graham Speaks." *Dance Observer* 30, no. 4 (1963): 53–55.

———. "A Modern Dancer's Primer for Action." Edited by Frederick R. Rogers. In *Dance: A Basic Educational Technique.* New York: Macmillan, 1941.

———. *The Notebooks of Martha Graham.* Introduction by Nancy Wilson Ross. New York: Harcourt, Brace, Jovanovich, 1973.

Horosko, Marian. "Martha Graham at 95." *Dance Magazine* (May 1989): 50–57.

Horosko, Marian, comp. *Martha Graham: The Evolution of Her Dance Theory and Training, 1926–1991.* Pennington, NJ: A Cappella Books, 1991.

Leatherman, Leroy. *Martha Graham: Portrait of the Lady as an Artist.* New York: Alfred A. Knopf, 1966.

McDonagh, Don. *Martha Graham.* New York: Praeger Publishers, 1974.

Morgan, Barbara. *Martha Graham: Sixteen Dances in Photographs.* New York: Duel, Sloan, and Pearce, 1941. Rev. ed. Dobbs Ferry, NY: Morgan & Morgan, 1980.

Sorell, Walter. "Two Rebels, Two Giants: Isadora and Martha." In Walter Sorell, ed., *The Dance Has Many Faces.* 2d ed. rev. New York: Columbia University Press, 1966.

Stodelle, Ernestine. *Deep Song: The Dance Story of Martha Graham.* New York, Schirmer Books; London, Collier Macmillan, 1984.

Terry, Walter. *Frontiers of Life: The Life of Martha Graham.* New York: Thomas Y. Crowell Co., 1975.

Tobias, Tobi. "A Conversation with Martha Graham." *Dance Magazine* (March 1984): 62–67.

Trowbridge, Charlotte. *Dance Drawings of Martha Graham.* Forward by Martha Graham; preface by James Johnson Sweeney. New York: Dance Observer, 1945.

Doris Humphrey

Cohen, Selma Jeanne. *Doris Humphrey: An Artist First.* Middletown, CT: Wesleyan University Press, 1972. Reprint. Pennington, NJ: Princeton Book Company, 1995.

Davis, Joan and Zelia Raye. "The Art of Doris Humphrey: An Appreciation by Zelia Raye and Joan Davis." The Dancing Times (Nov. 1931). Reprint. *The Dancing Times.* (Oct. 1990): 52–53.

Humphrey Centennial Issue. *Dance Research Journal* 28, no. 2 (Fall 1996).

Humphrey, Doris. "America's Modern Dance." In Myron Howard Nadel and Constance Gwen Nadel, eds., *The Dance Experience: Readings in Dance Appreciation.* New York: Praeger Publishers, 1970.

Humphrey, Doris. *The Art of Making Dances.* Edited by Barbara

Pollack. New York and Toronto: Rinehart & Company, Inc., 1959. Reprint. New York: Grove Press, 1962.

———, and Love, Paul. "The Dance of Doris Humphrey." In Virginia Stewart and Merle Armitage, eds., *The Modern Dance*. New York: E. Weyhe, 1935. (Brooklyn: Dance Horizons, 1970.)

———. "Dance Drama." In Walter Sorell, ed., *The Dance Has Many Faces*. 2d ed. rev. New York: Columbia University Press, 1966.

———. "New Dance: An Unfinished Autobiography." *Dance Perspectives*. 25 (1966).

Mindlin, Naomi, ed. Doris Humphrey: A Centennial Issue. *Choreography and Dance* (1997).

Schlundt, Christena L. "The Choreographer of Soaring: The Documentary Evidence." *Dance Chronicle* 6, no. 4 (1983): 363–373.

Siegel, Marcia B. *Days on Earth: The Dance of Doris Humphrey.* 1988. Reprint. Durham: Duke University Press, 1993.

Stodelle, Ernestine. *The Dance Technique of Doris Humphrey and Its Creative Potential*. Princeton, NJ: Princeton Book Company, Publishers, 1978.

Charles Weidman

Manasevit, Shirley D. "A Last Interview with Charles Weidman." *Dance Scope* 10, no. 1 (1975–1976): 32–50.

Nadira. "David and Goliath." *Arabesque* 19, no. 5 (Jan./Feb. 1994): 8–11.

Sherman, Jane. "Charles Weidman at Denishawn." *Ballet Review* 13, no. 3 (Fall 1985): 73–82.

Weidman, Charles. "Random Remarks." In Walter Sorell, ed., *The Dance Has Many Faces*. 2d ed. rev. New York: Columbia University Press, 1966.

———, and Love, Paul. "The Work of Charles Weidman." In Virginia Stewart and Merle Armitage, eds., *The Modern Dance*. New York: E. Weyhe, 1935. Reprint. Brooklyn: Dance Horizons, 1970.

Wynne, David. "Three Years With Charles Weidman." *Dance Perspectives* 60 (1974).

Hanya Holm

Cristofori, Marilyn. Hanya Holm Issue. *Choreography and Dance 2,* pt. 2 (1992).

———. "Hanya Holm, Portrait of a Pioneer." *Dance Teacher Now* 12, no. 4 (May 1990): 18–26.

Dudley, Jane. "The Early Life of an American Modern Dancer." *Dance Research* 10, no. 1 (Spring 1992): 3–20.

Holm, Hanya. "The German Dance in the American Scene." In Virginia Stewart and Merle Armitage, eds., *The Modern Dance*. New York: E. Weyhe, 1935. Reprint. Brooklyn: Dance Horizons, 1970.

——. "The Mary Wigman I Know." In Walter Sorell, ed., *The Dance Has Many Faces*. 2d ed. rev. New York: Columbia University Press, 1966.

Manning, Susan. "You Have to Hear What Isn't on the Surface: An Interview with Hanya Holm." *Ballett International* 16, no. 3 (Mar. 1993): 20–23.

Partsch-Bergsohn, Isa. "Hanya Holm: A Missing Link Between German and American Modern Dance." *Ballett International* 16, no. 3 (Mar. 1993): 14–17.

Siegel, Marcia B. "A Conversation with Hanya Holm." *Ballet Review* 9, no. 1 (Spring 1981): 5–30.

Sorell, Walter. *Hanya Holm: Biography of an Artist*. Middletown, CT: Wesleyan University Press, 1969.

Merce Cunningham

Adam, Judy, ed. *Dancers on a Plane/Cage Cunningham Johns*. New York: Alfred A Knopf; London: Thames & Hudson; in association with Anthony d'Offay Gallery, 1990.

Brown, Carolyn, et al. "Time to Walk in Space." *Dance Perspectives* 34 (1968).

Cunningham, Merce. *Changes: Notes on Choreography*. New York: Something Else Press, 1968.

——. "Choreography and the Dance." In Stanley Rosner and Lawrence E. Abt, eds., *The Creative Experience*. New York: Grossman Publications, 1970. Reprint. New York: Dell Publishing Co., 1972.

——. *The Dancer and the Dance/Conversations with Jacqueline Lesschaeve*. New York and London: Marion Boyars, 1985. Second (paperback) edition, 1991.

——. "The Function of a Technique for Dance." In Walter Sorell, ed., *The Dance Has Many Faces*. Cleveland and New York: World Publishing Co., 1951.

——. "The Impermanent Art." In Fernando Puma, ed., *Seven Arts 3*. Indian Hills, CO: Falcon's Riding Press, 1955.

——. "Story : Tale of a Dance and a Tour." *Dance Ink* 6, no. 1 (Spring 1995): 14–21.

Fischer, Eva Elisabeth. "Center is Everywhere." *Ballett International* 7, no. 6/7 (June/July 1984): 28–32.

Klosty, James, ed. *Merce Cunningham: Photographs*. New York: Proscenium Publishers, 1987.

———. *Merce Cunningham*. New York: Saturday Review Press, F. P. Dutton & Co., Inc., 1975.

Kostelanetz, Richard, ed. *Merce Cunningham: Dancing in Space and Time essay* 1944–1992. Pennington, NJ: A Cappella Books, 1992.

Snell, Michael. "Cunningham and the Critics." *Ballet Review* 3, no. 6 (1971): 16–39.

Yates, Peter. "Merce Cunningham Restores the Dance to Dance." *Impulse* (1965) pp- 13–17.

Erick Hawkins

Hawkins, Erick. *The Body is a Clear Place and Other Statements on Dance*. Princeton, NJ: Princeton Book Company, 1992.

———. "Erick Hawkins Addresses a New-to-Dance Audience." In Myron Howard Nadel and Constance Gwen Nadel, eds., *The Dance Experience: Readings in Dance Appreciation*. New York: Praeger Publishers, 1970.

———. "Pure Fact in Movement Technique and Choreography." *Dance Observer* 25, no. 9 (1958): 133–134.

———. Pure Poetry." In Selma Jeanne Cohen, ed., *The Modern Dance: Seven Statements of Belief*. Middletown, CT: Wesleyan University Press, 1965.

———. "What is the Most Beautiful Dance?" In Walter Sorell, ed., *The Dance Has Many Faces*. 2d ed. rev. New York: Columbia University Press, 1966.

———. "Why Does a Man Dance and What Does He Dance, and Who Should Watch Him?" In Myron Howard Nadel and Constance Gwen Nadel, eds., *The Dance Experience: Readings in Dance Appreciation*. New York: Praeger Publishers, 1970.

Norton, M. L. Gordon, ed. 5 *Essays on the Dance of Erick Hawkins*. New York: Foundation for Modern Dance, 1983.

Rochiem, Harvey. *Notes on Contemporary American Dance 1964*. Baltimore: University Extension Press, 1964.

José Limón

Hill, Martha. "José Limón and his Biblical works." *Choreography and Dance* 2, pt. 3 (1992): 57–61.

Lewis, Daniel. *The Illustrated Dance Technique of José Limón*. New York: Harper & Row, 1984.

Limón, José. "An American Accent." In Selma Jeanne Cohen, ed., *The Modern Dance: Seven Statements of Belief*. Middletown, CT: Wesleyan University Press, 1965.

———. "American Dance on Tour." *Juilliard Review* 6 (1958): 8–11.

———. "Composing a Dance." *Juilliard Review* 2 (1955): 17–23.

———. "Dancers Are Musicians Are Dancers." *Juilliard Review Annual* (1966–1967).

———. "Music Is the Strongest Ally to a Dancer's Way of Life." In Myron Howard Nadel and Constance Gwen Nadel, eds., *The Dance Experience Readings in Dance Appreciation*. New York: Praeger Publishers, 1970.

———. "On Dance." In Fernando Puma, ed., *Seven Arts* 1. Garden City, NY: Permabooks, Doubleday & Company, Inc., 1953.

———. "The Universities and the Arts." *Dance Scope* 1, no. 2 (1965): 23–27.

———. "The Virile Dance." In Walter Sorell, ed., *The Dance Has Many Faces*. 2d ed. rev. New York: Columbia University Press, 1966.

———. "Young Dancers State Their Views." *Dance Observer* 13, no. 1 (1946): 7.

Mindlin, Naomi. "José Limón's *The Moor's Pavane:* An Interview with Lucas Hoving." *Dance Research Journal*. New York: Congress on Research in Dance [CORD] 24, no. 1 (Spring 1992): 13–26.

Pollack, Barbara and Charles Humphrey Woodford. *Dance is a Moment: A Portrait of José Limón in Words and Pictures*. Pennington, NJ: Princeton Book Company, A Dance Horizons Book, 1993.

Siegel, Marcia B. "José Limón 1908–1972." *Ballet Review* 4, no. 4 (1973): 100–104.

Anna Sokolow

Garske, Rolf. "Life Gives the Subjects: Interview with Anna Sokolow." *Ballett International* 6, no. 6 (June 1983): 10–15, 49.

Sokolow, Anna. "Talking to Dance and Dancers." *Dance and Dancers* 5 (1967): 18–19.

Stodelle, Ernestine. "Anna Sokolow, Spokesman for the Psyche." *Ballet Review* 23, no. 1 (Spring 1995): 32–39.

Warren, Larry. *Anna Sokolow: The Rebellious Spirit*. Pennington, NJ: Princeton Book Company, 1991.

Winter, Rhoda. "Conversation with Anna Sokolow." *Impulse* (1958): 43–46.

Alwin Nikolais

Coleman, Martha. "On the Teaching of Choreography: An Interview with Alwin Nikolais." *Dance Observer* 17, no. 10 (1950): 148–150.

Conklin, J. L. "Alwin Nikolais." *Salome* 32/33 (1983): 50–57.

Copeland, Roger. "A Conversation with Alwin Nikolais." *Dance Scope* 8, no. 1 (1973–1974): 41–46.

Garske, Rolf. "Art Does Not Care What Form It Takes: Interview with Alwin Nikolais." *Ballett International* 13, no. 6–7 (June/July 1990): 23–29.

Louis, Murray. "The Contemporary Dance Theatre of Alwin Nikolais." *Dance Observer* 27, no. 2 (1960): 24–26.

Nikolais, Alwin. "An Art of Magic: Interview with Dance and Dancers." *Dance and Dancers* 7(1969): 24–26.

———. "A New Method of Dance Notation." In Myron Howard Nadel and Constance Gwen Nadel, eds., *The Dance Experience: Readings in Dance Appreciation*. New York: Praeger Publishers, 1970.

———. "Growth of a Theme." In Walter Sorell, ed., *The Dance Has Many Faces*. 2d ed. rev. New York: Columbia University Press, 1966.

———. "The New Dimension of Dance." *Impulse* (1958): 43–46.

———. "No Man from Mars." In Selma Jeanne Cohen, ed., *The Modern Dance Seven Statements of Belief* Middletown, CT: Wesleyan University Press, 1966.

———. "What Is the Most Beautiful Dance." In Walter Sorell, ed., *The Dance Has Many Faces*. Cleveland and New York: World Publishing Co., 1951.

Paul Taylor

Adams, Carolyn. "Lifeline to Taylor." *Ballet Review* 13, no. 4 (Winter 1986): 18–20.

Anderson, Jack. "Paul Taylor: Surface and Substance." *Ballet Review* 6, no. 1 (1977): 39–44.

Rosen, Lillie F. "Talking with Paul Taylor." *Dance Scope* 13, no. 2–3 (winter/spring 1979): 82–92.

Taylor, Paul. *Private Domain*. New York: Knopf, 1987.

———. "Another View: Portrait of the artist as Two Young Men." *Dance Magazine* (Jan. 1993): 64–69.

Alvin Ailey

Ailey, Alvin. *Revelations: The Autobiography of Alvin Ailey*. Secaucus, NJ: Carol Publishing Group, 1995.

———. with Arthur Todd. "Roots of the Blues." *Dance and Dancers* (Nov. 1961): 24–25.

Dunning, Jennifer. *Alvin Ailey: A Life in Dance*. Reading, MA: Addison-Wesley, 1996.

Sorell, Walter. "Style, Essence, Allusion." *Dance Magazine* (Aug 1963): 47, 62.

Muriel Topaz, ed. *Alvin Ailey: An American Visionary*. Choreography and Dance. Amsterdam: Harwood Academic Publishers, 1996.

Anna Halprin

Halprin, Anna. "Intuition and Improvisation." In Marian van Tuyl, ed., *Anthology of Impulse*. Brooklyn: Dance Horizons, 1969.

———. *Moving Toward Life: Five Decades of Transformational Dance*. Rachel Kaplan, ed. Middletown, CT: Wesleyan University Press, 1995.

———. "Yvonne Rainer Interviews Anna Halprin." *Drama Review* (T30), 10, no. 2 (1965): 168–178.

———, with illustrations by Charlene Koonce. *Movement Ritual I*. San Francisco: San Francisco Dancers' Workshop, 1979.

———, with Stinson, Allan. *Circle the Earth Manual: A Guide for Dancing Peace with the Planet*. Kentfield, CA: Tamalpa Institute, 1987.

Halprin, Lawrence. *The RSVP Cycles: Creative Processes in the Human Environment*. New York: George Braziller, Inc., 1969.

Judith Dunn

Dunn, Judith. "My Work and Judson's." *Ballet Review* 1, no. 6 (1967): 22–26.

Siegel, Marcia B., ed. "Dancer's Notes." *Dance Perspectives* 38 (1969).

Yvonne Rainer

Hecht, Robin Silver. "Reflections on the Career of Yvonne Rainer and the Values of Minimal Dance." *Dance Scope* 8, no. 1 (1973–1974): 12–25.

Rainer, Yvonne, et al. "Conversation in Manhattan." *Impulse* (1967): 57–64.

"The Dwarf Syndrome." In Walter Sorell, ed., *The Dance Has Many Faces*. 2d ed. rev. New York: Columbia University Press, 1966.

———. "Some Retrospective Notes on a Dance for 10 People and 12 Mattresses Called 'Parts of Some Sextets.'" *Tulane Drama Review* (T30) 10, no. 2 (1965): 142–166.

———. *Work, 1961–73*. Halifax: The Press of The Nova Scotia College of Art and Design; New York: New York University Press, 1974.

———. "Yvonne Rainer Interviews Anna Halprin." *Drama Review* (T30), 10, no. 2 (1965): 168–178.

Pilobolus

Fanger, Iris M. "Pilobolus." *Dance Magazine* 48, no. 7 (1974): 38–42.

Matson, Tim. *Pilobolus*. New York: Random House, 1978.

Trisha Brown

Brown, Trisha, et al. "Conversation in Manhattan." *Impulse* (1967): 57–64.

———. "Three Pieces." *Drama Review* (T65) 19, no. 1 (1975): 26–32.

Eigo, Jim. "Trisha Brown and Robert Rauschenberg." *Dance Ink* 5, no. 1 (Spring 1994): 22–25.

Hardy, Camille. "Trisha Brown: Pushing Post-Modern Art into Orbit." *Dance Magazine* (March 1985): [62]–66.

Siegel, Marcia B. "New Dance: Individuality, Image, and the Demise of the Coterie." *Dance Magazine* 48, no. 4 (1974): 39–44.

Sommer, Sally R. "Trisha Brown Making Dances." *Dance Scope* 11, no. 2 (1977): 7–18.

———. "The Sound of Movement." *Dance Ink* 4, no. 1 (Spring 1993): 4–6.

Douglas Dunn

Dunn, Douglas. "Notes on Playing Myself." *Eddy* 4 (1974): 22.

———. "Interview." *Semiotext(e)* 3, no. 2 (1978): 204–214.

———. "Fearing." *Contact Quarterly* 19, no. 2 (1994): 102–103.

———. "Going to Meet Cougar-Asleep-on-Tree-Branch." *New Literary History* 26, no. 1 (1995): 73–96.

Rod Rodgers

Rodgers, Rod. "For the Celebration of Our Blackness." *Dance Scope* 3, no. 2 (1967): 6–10.

———. "Is it Just for Jobs?" *Dance Magazine* 41, no. 4 (1967): 26.

———. "Men and Dance: Why Do We Question the Image?" *Dance Magazine* 40, no. 4 (1966): 35–36.

Stevens, Larry. "Rod Rodgers: Man on the Move." *Dance Pages* 2, no. 2 (Fall 1984): 20–22.

Twyla Tharp

Kerner, Mary. "Twyla Tharp: New Role." *Dance Teacher Now* 11, no. 5 (June 1989): 14–18.

Twyla Tharp. *Push Comes to Shove.* New York: Bantam, 1992.

——— "Space, Jazz, Pop and All that Stuff." *Dance and Dancers* (May 1974): 28–31.

Mark Morris

Acocella, Joan. *Mark Morris.* New York: Farrar Straus Giroux, 1993

Siebert, Charles. "Footloose!" *Esquire* (December 1985): 142–150.

Tobias, Tobi. "All Grown Up: Mark Morris." *New York Magazine* (Dec. 11, 1995): 56–60.

———. "Manchild in the Promised Land: Mark Morris." *Dance Magazine* (Dec. 1984).

Vaughan, David. " A Conversation with Mark Morris." *Ballet Review* (Summer 1986): 26–36.

Mary Fulkerson

Crickmay, Chris. "Fragments of Daily Life : Mary Fulkerson's World of Images and Compositional Ideas." *Contact Quarterly* 13, no. 2 (Spring/Summer 1988): 9–18.

Fulkerson, Mary O'Donnell. "Moving for Performance." *New Dance* 32 (Spring 1985): 12, 17.

———. "Responsible Anarchy." *Ballett International/Tanzaktuell* 8 (Aug./Sept. 1994): 29–32.

New Dance Collective. "Mary Fulkerson: An Interview." *New Dance* 7 (Summer 1978): 12–14.

Molissa Fenley

Dillon, James. "Molissa Fenley: Removing the Post-Modern Label." *Dance Magazine* (Oct 1983): 67–69.

Fenley, Molissa. "Engram." *Drama Review* 27, no. 4, T100 (Winter 1983): 38–39.

Gruen, John. "Molissa Fenley: A Separate Voice." *Dance Magazine* (May 1991): 38–41.

Skurdall, Cheri. "Interview with Molissa Fenley." *Women & Performance* 2, no. 1 (1984): 101–105.

Bill T. Jones

Jones, Bill T., with Peggy Gillespie. *Last Night on Earth*. New York: Pantheon Books, 1995.

Quasha, Susan and Elizabeth Zimmer, eds. *Body Against Body: The Dance and Other Collaborations of Bill T. Jones & Arnie Zane*. Barrytown, NY: Station Hill Press, 1989.

Ricketts, Raymond Julian. "Working with Bill T. Jones." *Dance Now* 4, no. 3 (Autumn 1995): 47–53.

Tegeder, Ulrich. "Bill T. Jones & Arnie Zane: Interview." *Ballett International* 7, no. 9 (Sept 1984): 19–21.

Wallach, Maya. "A Conversation with Bill T. Jones." *Ballet Review* 18, no. 4 (Winter 1990–1991): 73–75.

David Gordon

Gordon, David, Nancy Stark Smith and Valda Setterfield. "David Gordon & Valda Setterfield, Part 2: Talking about Making Work, Not Making Work, Teaching and More." *Contact Quarterly* 4, no. 3/4 (Spring/Summer 1979): 8–11.

Banes, Sally. "An Interview with David Gordon." *Eddy* 9 (Winter 1977): 17–25.

Garth Fagan

Fagan, Garth. "Time After Before Place." In Selma Jeanne Cohen, ed., *Dance As a Theatre Art.: Source Readings in Dance History from 1581 to the Present.* 2d ed. With new section by Katy Matheson. Princeton, NJ: Princeton Book Company, 1992, pp. 246–250.

Mason, Francis. "A Conversation with Garth Fagan." *Ballet Review* 23, no. 1 (Spring 1995): 18–28.

Vaughan, David. "Garth Fagan Dance: Discipline is freedom." *Dance Magazine* (Nov. 1990): 40–43.

Lucinda Childs

Childs, Lucinda. "Interview." *Contemporary Dance.* New York: Abbeville Press, 1978, pp. 58–81.

———. "Notes: '64–'74." *The Drama Review,* Post-modern dance issue 19, no. 1 (Mar 1975): 33–36.

Constanti, Sophie. "Swimming Against the Tide." *Dance Theatre Journal* 8, no. 4 (Spring 1991): 6–8.

Eiko & Koma

Josa-Jones, Paula. "Delicious Moving." *Contact Quarterly* 11, no. 1 (Winter 1986): 11–15.

Mihopoulos, Effie. "Eiko and Koma: Interview with the Dance Duo Eiko and Koma, Feb. 9, 1983." *Salome* 32/33 (1983): 91–105.

Windham, Leslie. "A Conversation with Eiko & Koma." *Ballet Review* 16, no. 2 (Summer 1988): 47–59.

Deborah Hay

Hay, Deborah. "The Grand Dance." *Contact Quarterly* 7, no. 2 (Winter 1982): 39–42.

———. *Lamb at the Altar: The Story of a Dance.* Durham, N.C.: Duke University Press, 1994.

———. *Moving Through the Universe in Bare Feet: Ten Circle Dances for Everybody.* Chicago: Swallow Press, 1975.

———. "Playing Awake: Letters to My Daughter." *Drama Review* 33, no. 4 (Winter 1989): 23–27.

———. "Stretching the Practice." *Contact Quarterly* 16, no. 1 (Winter 1991): 13–16.

Jowale Willa Jo Zollar

Sims, Lowery Stokes. "Heat and Other Climatic Manifestations: Urban Bush Women, Thought Music and Craig Harris with the Dirty Tones Band." *High Performance* #45 (Spring 1989).

Zollar, Jawole Willa Jo. "Listen: Our History is Shouting at Us."
   Update Dance/USA 8, no. 3 (Nov./Dec. 1990): 16–18.

II Topics

Choreography

Blom, Lynne Anne, and L. Tarin. *The Intimate Act of Choreography.*
   Pittsburgh, PA: University of Pittsburgh Press, 1982.

Cunningham, Merce. *Changes: Notes on Choreography.* New York:
   Something Else Press, 1968.

Ellfeldt, Lois V. *A Primer for Choreographers.* Palo Alto, CA: National
   Press Books, 1967.

Gray, Miriam, ed. *Focus on Dance* V. Washington, D. C.: American
   Association for Health, Physical Education and Recreation, 1969.

Hawkins, Alma M. *Creating Through Dance.* Englewood Cliffs, NJ:
   Prentice-Hall, Inc., 1966. Reprint. Princeton, NJ: Princeton Book
   Company, 1988.

———. *Moving from Within: A New Method for Dance Making.*
   Pennington, NJ: A Cappella Books, 1991.

Hayes, Elizabeth R. *Dance Composition and Production for High Schools
   and Colleges.* New York: Dance Horizons, 1981. 2d ed. Pennington,
   NJ: Princeton Book Company, 1993.

Horst, Louis. *Modern Forms In Relation to the Other Arts.* With Carol
   Russell. San Francisco: Impulse Publications, 1961, 1963. Reprint.
   Pennington, NJ: Princeton Book Company, 1987.

———. *Pre-Classic Forms.* New York: Kamin Dance Publishers, 1953.
   Reprint. Brooklyn: Dance Horizons, 1968. Reprint. Pennington,
   NJ: Princeton Book Company, 1987.

Humphrey, Doris. *The Art of Making Dances.* Edited by Barbara
   Pollack. New York and Toronto: Rinehart & Company, Inc., 1959.
   Reprint. New York: Grove Press, 1962. Reprint. Pennington, NJ:
   Princeton Book Company, 1987.

Lavender, Larry. *Dancers Talking Dance: Critical Evaluation in the
   Choreography Class.* Champaign, IL: Human Kinetics, 1996.

Preston-Dunlop, Valerie. *Point of Departure: The Dancer's Space.*
   London: Valerie Preston-Dunlop, 1984.

Turner, Margery J. *New Dance: Approaches to Nonliteral Choreography.*
   With Ruth Grauert and Arlene Zallman. Pittsburgh: University of
   Pittsburgh Press, 1971.

Winearls, Jane. *Choreography: The Art of the Body: An Anatomy of
   Expression.* London: Dance Books, 1990.

Criticism

Croce, Arlene. *Afterimages.* New York: Alfred A. Knopf, 1978.

Denby, Edwin. *Looking at the Dance.* New York: Horizon Press, 1968.

Gere, David, Lewis Segal, Patrice Clark Koelsch, and Elizabeth Zimmer, eds. *Looking Out: Perspectives on Dance and Criticism in a Multicultural World/Dance Critics Association.* New York: Schirmer Books; London: Prentice Hall International, 1995.

Jowitt, Deborah. *Dance Beat: Selected Views and Reviews 1967–1976.* New York: Marcel Dekker, Inc., 1977.

Morris, Gay, ed. *Moving Words: Re-writing Dance.* London; New York : Routledge, 1996.

Siegel, Marcia B. *At the Vanishing Point.* New York: Saturday Review Press, 1972.

———. *The Shapes of Change/Images of American Dance.* Boston: Houghton Mifflin, 1979.

———. *Watching the Dance Go By.* New York: Houghton Mifflin Co., 1977.

Films

Spain, Louise, ed. *Dance on Camera: A Guide to Dance Films and Videos.* New York: Neal-Schuman Publishers, Inc. and Lanham, MD and London: The Scarecrow Press, Inc., 1997.

History

Anderson, Jack. *Art Without Boundaries.* Iowa City, IA: University of Iowa Press, 1997.

———. *Ballet & Modern Dance: A Concise History.* Princeton, NJ: Princeton Book Company, 1986. 2d ed. Pennington, NJ: Princeton Book Company, 1992.

———. *Dance.* New York: Newsweek Books, 1974.

Armitage, Merle. *Dance Memoranda.* Edited by Edwin Corle. New York: Duell, Sloan and Pearce, 1949.

Au, Susan. *Ballet & Modern Dance.* London; New York: Thames and Hudson, 1988.

Banes, Sally. *Democracy's Body: Judson Dance Theater, 1962–1964.* Durham, NC: Duke University Press, 1993.

———. *Terpsichore in Sneakers: Post-Modern Dance.* Boston: Houghton Mifflin Company, 1980. Reprint. Middletown, CT: Wesleyan University Press.

———. *Writing Dancing in the Age of Postmodernism.* Hanover, NH: University Press of New England, 1994.

Clarke, Mary and Clement Crisp. *The History of Dance.* New York: Crown Publishers, 1981.

Cohen, Selma Jeanne, ed. *Dance as a Theatre Art*. New York: Dodd, Mead and Co., 1974. Second ed., with a new section by Katy Matheson. Princeton, NJ: Princeton Book Company, 1992.

Copeland, Roger. "Founding Mothers: Duncan, Graham, Rainer and Sexual Politics." *Dance Theatre Journal* 8, no. 3 (Autumn 1990): 6–9.

de Mille, Agnes. *The Book of the Dance*. New York: Golden Press, 1963.

Dunn, Robert Ellis. "Judson Days." *Contact Quarterly*14, no. 1 (Winter 1989): 9–13.

Emery, Lynne Fauley. *Black Dance in the United States from 1619 to 1970*. Palo Alto, CA: National Press Books, 1972.

Hering, Doris. *Twenty-Five Years of American Dance*. Rev. ed. New York: Rudolf Orthwine, 1954.

Highwater, Jamake. *Dance: Rituals of Experience*. Pennington, NJ: Princeton Book Company, 1992.

Jonas, Gerald. *Dancing: The Pleasure, Power, and Art of Movement*. New York: H.N. Abrams, in association with Thirteen/WNET, 1992.

Jowitt, Deborah. *Time and the Dancing Image*. New York: W. Morrow, 1988.

Kaplan, Peggy Jarrell. *Portraits of Choreographers*. New York: R. Feldman Fine Arts; Paris : Editions Bougé, 1988.

Kirstein, Lincoln. *Dance: A Short History of Classical Theatrical Dancing*. New York: G. P. Putnam & Sons, 1935. Reprint. Brooklyn: Dance Horizons, 1974. Reprint. Pennington, NJ: Princeton Book Company, 1987.

Kraus, Richard, Sarah Chapman Hilsendager and Brenda Dixon. *History of the Dance in Art and Education*. 3d ed. Englewood Cliffs, NJ: Prentice Hall, 1991. Originally published as Kraus, Richard. History of the Dance. Englewood Cliffs, NJ: Prentice-Hall, Inc., 1969.

Kriegsman, Sali Ann. *Modern Dance in America: The Bennington Years*. Boston: G. K. Hall, 1981.

Laine, Barry. "In Search of Judson." *Dance Magazine* (Sept 1982): 80–84.

Lloyd, Margaret. *The Borzoi Book of Modern Dance*. New York: Alfred A. Knopf, 1949. Reprint. Brooklyn: Dance Horizons, 1970. Reprint. Pennington, NJ: Princeton Book Company, 1987.

McDonagh, Don. *The Complete Guide to Modern Dance*. Garden City, NY: Doubleday & Co., Inc., 1976. (New York: Popular Library, 1977.)

———. *The Rise and Fall and Rise of Modern Dance*. New York: Outer-bridge and Dienstfrey, 1970. Reprint. New York: New American

Library, Inc., 1971. Rev. ed. Pennington, NJ: A Cappella Books, 1990.

Magriel, Paul. *Chronicles of the American Dance.* New York: Henry Holt & Co., 1948.

Martin, John. *America Dancing.* New York: Dodge Publishing Co., 1936. Reprint. Brooklyn: Dance Horizons, 1968.

———. *The Dance.* New York: Tudor Publishing Company, 1946.

———. *The Dance in Theory.* Reprint. Princeton, NJ : Princeton Book Company, 1989.

———. *Introduction to the Dance.* New York: A. S. Barnes, 1933. Reprint. Brooklyn: Dance Horizons, 1965.

———. *John Martin's Book of the Dance.* New York: Tudor Publishing Co., 1963.

Maynard, Olga. *American Modern Dancers: The Pioneers.* Boston and Toronto: Little, Brown and Co., 1965.

Mazo, Joseph H. *Prime Movers: The Makers of Modern Dance in America.* New York: William Morrow and Co., Inc., 1977. Reprint. Princeton, NJ : Princeton Book Company, 1982.

Owen, Norton, and Jane Sherman. "Martha Graham & Ted Shawn." *Dance Magazine* (July 1995): 42–45.

Palmer, Winthrop. *Theatrical Dancing in America.* New York: Bernard Ackerman, 1945. 2d ed. rev. New York: A. S. Barnes and Co., 1978.

Prickett, Stacey. "From Workers' Dance to New Dance." *Dance Research* 7, no. 1 (Spring 1989): 47–64.

Savery, Helen. "Dancing in the Depression." *Dance Chronicle* 7, no. 3 (1984–85): 279–293.

Schaik, Eva van. "Terpsichore and Her Memory: The Image of the Female Dancer." *Ballett International* 13, no. 3 (Mar. 1990): 17–24.

Sherman, Jane. *The Drama of Denishawn Dance.* Middletown, CT: Wesleyan University Press, 1979.

———. "Martha and Doris in Denishawn: A Closer Look." *Dance Chronicle* 17, no. 2 (1994): 179–193.

———. *Soaring.* Middletown, CT: Wesleyan University Press, 1976.

Siegel, Marcia B. *The Shapes of Change: Images of American Dance.* Boston: Houghton Mifflin Co., 1979.

Sorell, Walter. *Dance in its Time.* Garden City, NY: Anchor Press/Doubleday, 1981.

———. *The Dance Through the Ages.* New York: Grosset and Dunlap, 1967.

Stebbins, Genevieve. *The Delsarte System of Expression.* Brooklyn: Dance Horizons, 1978.

Terry, Walter. *The Dance in America.* New York: Harper and Bros.,

1956. Rev. ed. New York: Harper & Row, 1973.

———. *I Was There: Selected Dance Reviews and Articles, 1936–1976.* Compiled and edited by Andrew Mark Wentink. New York: Marcel Dekker Press, 1978.

Trager, Philip. *Dancers.* Boston: Little, Brown, 1992.

Warren, Larry. *Lester Horton: Modern Dance Pioneer.* New York: Marcel Dekker Press, 1977.

Theory

Arnheim, Rudolf. *Toward a Psychology of Art.* Berkeley and Los Angeles: University of California Press, 1967.

Cage, John. *Silence.* Middletown, CT: Wesleyan University Press, 1961.

Cohen, Selma Jeanne, ed. *The Modern Dance: Seven Statements of Belief* Middletown, CT: Wesleyan University Press, 1966.

———. *Next Week, Swan Lake: Reflections on Dance and Dances.* Middletown, CT: Wesleyan University Press, 1982.

Copeland, Roger and Marshall Cohen, eds. *What is Dance?: Readings in Theory and Criticism.* Oxford [Oxfordshire]; New York: Oxford University Press, 1983.

Daly, Ann, ed. "What has Become of Postmodern Dance?" *Drama Review* 36, no. 1 (T133) (Spring 1992): 48–69.

Forti, Simone. *Handbook in Motion.* Halifax, Canada: The Press of the Nova Scotia College of Art and Design, 1973.

Hanna, Judith Lynne. *To Dance is Human: A Theory of Nonverbal Communication.* Austin: University of Texas Press, 1979. Reprint. Chicago: University of Chicago Press, 1987.

H'Doubler, Margaret. *Dance: A Creative Art Experience.* New York: Appleton. Century. Crofts, 1940. Reprints. Madison: University of Wisconsin Press, 1959, 1966.

Kinney, Troy. *The Dance: Its Place in Art and Life.* New York: F. A. Stokes Co., 1924.

Kreemer, Connie. *Further Steps: Fifteen Choreographers on Modern Dance.* New York: Harper & Row, 1987.

Langer, Suzanne K. *Feeling and Form.* New York: Charles Scribner's Sons, 1953.

———. *Problems of Art.* New York: Charles Scribner's Sons, 1957.

———. *Reflections on Art.* Baltimore: John Hopkins University Press, 1959.

Livet, Anne, ed. *Contemporary Dance.* New York: Abbeville Press, Inc., 1978.

Louis, Murray. *Inside Dance: Essays.* New York: St. Martin's Press, 1980.

Lyle, Cynthia. *Dancers on Dancing.* New York and London: Drake Publishers, 1977.

Martin, John. *The Modern Dance.* New York: A. S. Barnes Co., 1936. Reprint. Brooklyn: Dance Horizons, 1965.

Nadel, Myron Howard, and Nadel, Constance Gwen, eds. *The Dance Experience: Readings in Dance Appreciation.* New York: Praeger Publishers, 1970.

Percival, John. *Experimental Dance.* New York: Universe Books, 1971.

Rogers, Frederick Rand. *Dance, a Basic Educational Technique.* 1941. New York: Dance Horizons, 1980.

Rogosin, Elinor. *The Dance Makers: Conversations with American Choreographers.* New York: Walker, 1980.

Selden, Elizabeth. *The Dancer's Quest.* Berkeley and Los Angeles: University of California Press, 1935.

———. *Elements of the Free Dance.* New York: A. S. Barnes, 1930.

Sheets, Maxine. *The Phenomenology of Dance.* Madison: University of Wisconsin Press, 1966.

Sorell, Walter, ed. *The Dance Has Many Faces.* Cleveland and New York: World Publishing Co., 1951. 2d ed. rev. New York: Columbia University Press, 1966.

———. *The Dancer's Image: Points and Counterpoints.* New York: Columbia University Press, 1971.

Stewart, Virginia, and Armitage, Merle, eds. *The Modern Dance.* New York: F. Weyhe, 1935. Reprint. Brooklyn: Dance Horizons, 1970.

van Tuyl, Marian, ed. *Anthology of Impulse.* Brooklyn: Dance Horizons, 1970.

von Laban, Rudolf. *Choreutics.* Edited by Lisa Ullman. London: MacDonald & Evans, 1966.

———, and Lawrence, F. C. *Effort.* London: MacDonald & Evans, 1947.

———. *A Life For Dance.* New York: Theatre Arts Books, 1975.

———. *The Mastery of Movement.* 2d ed. London: MacDonald & Evans, 1960.

———. *Principles of Dance and Movement Notation.* London: MacDonald & Evans, 1956.

Reference Material

Adshead, Janet and June Layson. *Dance History: A Methodology for Study.* London: Dance Books, 1983.

Brack, Clairette and Irina Wuyts, eds. *Dance and Research: An Interdisciplinary Approach.* Proceedings of the International Congress "Dance and Research", July 2–6, 1989, Vrije Universiteit Brussel, Brussels, Belgium. Louvain : Peeters Press, 1991.

Clarke, Mary, and Vaughan, David, eds., *The Encyclopedia of Dance and*

Ballet. New York: G. P. Putnam's Sons, 1977.

Chujoy, Anatole. *Dance Encyclopedia*. New York: A. S. Barnes and Co. Inc., 1949. Rev. and enlarged by Anatole Chujoy and P. W. Manchester. New York: Simon and Schuster, 1967.

Kaprelian, Mary H., comp. and ed. *Aesthetics for Dancers: A Selected Annotated Bibliography*. Washington, D. C.: American Alliance for Health, Physical Education and Recreation, 1976.

Love, Paul. *Modern Dance Terminology*. New York: Kamin Dance Publishers, 1952. Reprint with a New Introduction by Eleanor King. Pennington, NJ: Princeton Book Company, 1997.

McDonagh, Don. *The Complete Guide to Modern Dance*. Garden City, NY: Doubleday & Co. Inc., 1976.

New York Public Library. *Dance Collection Catalogue*. Online via the internet, updated daily.

New York Public Library. *Dance on Disc: Catalogue of the Dance Collection of the New York Public Library*. New York: The New York Public Library, Astor, Lenox, and Tilden Foundation, distributed by G. K. Hall & Co., an imprint of Macmillan Publishing USA, a division of Simon & Shuster, issued annually.

SELECTED
VIDEOGRAPHY

Most videos listed below can be ordered through Princeton Book Company, Publishers at 1–800–220–7149

Air for the G String. Choreography by Doris Humphrey. Analysis and Coaching by Ernestine Stodelle. 120 minutes, color, 1997. Dance Horizons Video release, Pennington, NJ.

Anna Sokolow, Choreographer. Directed by Lucille Rhodes and Margaret Murphy. 20 minutes, filmed in 1978, color, 1991. Dance Horizons Video release, Pennington, NJ.

Baryshnikov Dances Sinatra. Starring Mikhail Baryshnikov and members of the ABT. 60 minutes, color, stereo, 1985. Distributed by Kultur, West Long Branch, NJ.

Bill T. Jones: Dancing to the Promised Land. Performed by the Bill T. Jones/Arnie Zane Dance Co. 60 minutes, color, 1994. Distributed by V.I.E.W. Video, New York.

Bolero and Pictures at an Exhibition. Choreography by Lar Lubovitch and Moses Pendleton. 66 minutes, color, 1994. Distributed by Music Video Distributors, Norristown, PA.

Cage/Cunningham. 95 minutes, color, filmed in 1991. Distributed by Kultur, West Long Branch, NJ.

Charles Weidman: On His Own. Narrated by Alwin Nikolais. 60 minutes, color & b&w, 1990. Dance Horizons Video release, Pennington, NJ.

Contemporary Dance Training I, Off Center: A Step Into Modern Dance with Phyllis Gutelius. 25 minutes, color, 1989. Distributed by GGE Productions, Geismar, LA.

Contemporary Dance Training II, The Class, Do It! with Phyllis Gutelius. 65 minutes, color, 1989. Distributed by GGE Productions, Geismar, LA.

Dance and Myth: The World of Jean Erdman. Part I: The Early Dances. 53 minutes; Part II: The Group Dances, 59 minutes; Part III: The Later Solos, 67 minutes. Color, 1995. Distributed by Unimix Entertainment, New York.

Dance Black America. Narrated by Geoffrey Holder. 87 minutes, filmed in 1983, color, 1990. Dance Horizons Video release, Pennington, NJ.

The Dance Works of Doris Humphrey: With My Red Fires and New Dance. Choreographed by Doris Humphrey; Performed by the American Dance Festival Company. 60 minutes, filmed in 1972, color, 1989. Dance Horizons Video release, Pennington, NJ.

Dancing. Eight-part, multicultural series filmed in locations around the world, first shown on PBS in May 1993. Approximately 60 minutes per tape. Distributed by Kultur, West Long Branch, NJ.

Denishawn: The Birth of Modern Dance. 40 minutes, color/b&w, 1988. Distributed by Kultur, West Long Branch, NJ.

Doris Humphrey Technique: The Creative Potential. Written, directed, and hosted by Ernestine Stodelle. 45 minutes, color/b&w, 1992. Dance Horizons Video release, Pennington, NJ.

Erick Hawkins' America. Performed by the Erick Hawkins Dance Company. 57 minutes, color, 1992. Dance Horizons Video release, Pennington, NJ.

European Dance Theater. Produced by Isa Partsch-Bergsohn. Directed by Hal Bergsohn, 62 minutes, color/black & white, 1997. Dance Horizons Video release, Pennington, NJ.

An Evening with Alvin Ailey. With the Alvin Ailey American Dance Theatre. 108 minutes, color, 1986. Distributed by Kultur, West Long Branch, NJ.

Five Dances by Martha Graham. Performed by Martha Graham Dance Company. 86 minutes, color, 1996. Distributed by Music Video Distributors, Norristown, PA.

Griot New York. Choreography by Garth Fagan, featuring Garth Fagan Dance and the Wynton Marsalis Septet. 87 minutes, color, 1995. Distributed by Music Video Distributors, Norristown, PA.

Hanya: Portrait of a Pioneer. The Story of Dancer/Choreographer Hanya Holm. Hosted by Julie Andrews and Alfred Drake. 60 minutes, color, 1988. Dance Horizons Video release, Pennington, NJ.

The Hard Nut. Choreography by Mark Morris, performed by Mark Morris Dance Group. 87 minutes, color, 1992. Distributed by Music Video Distributors, Norristown, PA.

Intensive Course in Elementary Labanotation. By Jill Beck, Ph.D. Five 120-minute videocassettes, color, 30 pages supplementary booklet. Dance Horizons Video release, Pennington, NJ.

Isadora Duncan Dance. Technique and repertory performed by the Isadora Duncan Dance Ensemble directed by Julia Levien and Andrea Mantell Seidel. 60 minutes, color, 1994. Dance Horizons Video release, Pennington, NJ.

Journey Through Dance with Gay Cheney. 73 minutes, color, 1995. Dance Horizons Video release, Pennington, NJ.

Lester Horton Technique: The Warm-Up. Ana Marie Forsythe and Marjorie Perces, Artistic Directors. 45 minutes, color, 1990. Distributed by Kultur, West Long Branch, NJ.

Martha Graham: The Dancer Revealed. Narrated by Claire Bloom. 60 minutes, color, 1994. Distributed by Kultur, West Long Branch, NJ.

Martha Graham: In Performance. 93 minutes, b&w, first video release 1988. Distributed by Kultur, West Long Branch, NJ.

Mary Wigman: 1886–1973. Narration by Mary Wigman, with voice-over in English. 41 minutes, b&w, 1990. Dance Horizons Video release, Pennington, NJ.

The Men Who Danced: The Story of Ted Shawn's Male Dancers, 1933–1940. 30 minutes, produced in 1986, color with b&w historical footage, 1990. Dance Horizons Video release, Pennington, NJ.

Murray Louis in Concert: Dance Solos. Choreography by Murray Louis. 45 minutes, filmed 1972–1988, color, 1989. Dance Horizons Video release, Pennington, NJ.

Points in Space. Merce Cunningham Dance Company. 55 minutes, color, VHS HiFi, 1986. Distributed by Kultur, West Long Branch, NJ.

Speaking in Tongues. Choreography by Paul Taylor, performed by the Paul Taylor Company. 54 minutes, color, 1991. Distributed by Music Video Distributors, Norristown, PA.

Three by Martha Graham. With the Martha Graham Dance Company (1965, 1967, 1969). 87 minutes, color, 1996. Distributed by Pyramid Home Video, Santa Monica, CA.

A Tribute to Alvin Ailey. Features the Alvin Ailey American Dance Theatre. 120 minutes, color, 1992. Distributed by Kultur, West Long Branch, NJ.

The World of Alwin Nikolais. Directed and Narrated by Murray Louis, 5 different programs. Color, 1996. Distributed by Murray Louis Studio, New York.

The Wrecker's Ball. Three Dances by Paul Taylor with the Paul Taylor Dance Company. 56 minutes, color, 1996. Distributed by Forward Marketing.

Index